DISCA T3-AJK-781

12.30'

# THE REALM OF SPIRIT
## AND
# THE REALM OF CAESAR

# THE REALM OF SPIRIT
# AND
# THE REALM OF CAESAR

by

## NICOLAS BERDYAEV

Translated by
## DONALD A. LOWRIE

HARPER & BROTHERS, PUBLISHERS, NEW YORK

*197*
*B486r*

*Library of Congress catalogue card number: 53-5002*

# CONTENTS

# PUBLISHER'S FOREWORD
(from the Russian original)

THE PUBLICATION OF this last work of Berdyaev represents a collective effort by a small group of the great philosopher's friends on whose initiative the Berdyaev Society has been founded. The manuscript was in such a state that it required the work of four different persons intimately associated with Berdyaev to reduce it to a script which could be presented to the printer. Those responsible were: Mme. E. Rapp, Mme. T. Klepinine, Mr. J. P. Kazatchkine and Mr. S. P. Zhaba.

Y.M.C.A. PRESS,
   PARIS.
1951.

# TRANSLATOR'S PREFACE

A TRANSLATOR MAY DECIDE to produce a smooth, "literary" version, more or less an interpretation, or he may attempt to reproduce in the new language, the author's own style, giving as nearly literal a reproduction as is compatible with a readable and understandable text. The latter course has been chosen for this translation. Save for some division into paragraphs and rare additions of connective or transitional words, this is just as Berdyaev wrote it, with his somewhat staccato style (the gush of his thoughts is too rapid to be caught in the small dipper of his pen), his frequent repetition of a given word, even the words he invents himself, sometimes almost impossible of translation.

D. A. L.

PARIS.
MAY, 1952.

# THE REALM OF SPIRIT
## AND
# THE REALM OF CAESAR

# THE STRUGGLE FOR THE TRUTH
## (A gnosseological introduction)

WE LIVE IN A time when men neither love nor seek the truth. In ever greater measure, truth is being replaced by the will to power, by what is useful or valuable to special interests. This lack of love for the truth appears not only in nihilistic or sceptic attitudes toward it, but in substituting for it some sort of faith or dogmatic doctrine in whose name falsehood is permitted, falsehood which is considered not evil, but good. Indifference to the truth was manifest long ago in dogmatic beliefs which prevented the free search for it. Science developed in the European world as free investigation and search for truth, quite independent of its value or usefulness. But later science, too, began to be used as a weapon of anti-religious doctrines such as Marxism or technocracy. And if our times are distinguished by an exceptional tendency to lying, it is a special sort of untruth. Falsehood is affirmed as some holy duty for the sake of higher purposes. Evil is justified in the name of good. This, of course, is not new. History has always tended to justify evil for her own higher purposes. (Hegel's "cunning of reason".) But in our time this process has attained enormous dimensions, and it is something new in philosophy, that the very idea of truth has been shaken. It is true that the forerunners in this negation of the truth were the ancient Sophists, but they were soon overcome by Plato, Aristotle, Plotinus—all the summits of Greek thought. The views of truth held by the empiricists and the positivists were vague and contradictory, but in reality even they recognized its undoubtability, as well as did the opposing philosophic tendencies, for which truth was absolute. Doubt of the old concept of truth began with pragmatic philosophy, but in a form neither radical nor permanent. The shock to truth in Marx and Nietzsche was of vastly greater significance, although the two shook the truth from opposite directions. Marx asserts the historic relativism of truths, as a weapon in the class-struggle, based on dialectic borrowed from Hegel. The dialectic lie, widely practised by Marxists, is justified by dialectic materialism, which, in flat contradiction to its philosophical bases, is finally hailed as truth absolute. And to this truth revealed by Marxism we find a dogmatic attitude resembling that of the Catholic Church to its dogmas. But Marxist philosophy, which is a philosophy of the practical, considers truth as a weapon for the struggle of the revolutionary proletariat, for whom truth is something different than for the bourgeois classes, even when they are dealing with the truths of natural science.

Nietszche understood truth as the expression of the struggle for the will to power, as a created value; truth is made subordinate to the creation of a race of super-men. In reality, the irrational philosophy of life is not interested in truth, although in this philosophy there is a grain of truth, the truth that knowledge is a function of life. More interesting is existential philosophy, pregnant with the future, inclined to assert, not the old objectivized concept of truth, but a subjective-existential concept.

But this is not a denial of truth. In Kirkegaard absolute truth is revealed in the subjective and individual. In this connection the latest tendencies in existentialist philosophy are very contradictory. In his pamphlet devoted to the problem of truth, Heidegger, who must be called an existentialist philosopher, inclines toward an ontologic and objective concept of truth. But his classic conception of truth is expressed in new terminology, original and more refined. In the final analysis of Heidegger's thought, it is incomprehensible why man (Dasein) can come to know truth. Basing truth on freedom contradicts the ontological understanding of truth, in which the centre of gravity lies in revealed existence. In contrast to other existentialists, Heidegger holds to the old conception of truth, only expresses it in a new fashion. In wide circles of the philosophically naïve we see the triumph of relativism and historism in which there is a bit of truth, but which also contains a large dose of fundamental falsehood. Historism is unable to understand the meaning of history, since it rejects meaning in general. In politics, which play such a dominant role in our times, people generally do not talk of truth and falsehood, of good or evil, but of "right" and "left," of reaction or revolution, although criteria of this kind are beginning to lose all meaning. The chaos into which the world is now plunged, and along with the world its thought, should lead to a comprehension of the indissoluble bond between Truth and the Logos meaning. Dialectic loses all its meaning if there is no Meaning, no Logos which must prevail in dialectic development. This is why dialectic materialism is a contradiction of terms. Historic development which gives birth to relativism is impossible if there is no Logos, no Meaning for historic development. And this meaning cannot be contained in the process of development itself. We shall see that the old, static, objectivized concept of truth is false and has called forth a reaction which has gone so far as to deny truth. But even in the subjective-existentialist, dynamic concept of truth, it remains constant and takes on another meaning: Finally, in the deepest depths it is revealed that truth, integral truth, is God, that truth is not the relationship or the identity of the comprehending, judging subject with objective reality, with objective being, but rather is entrance into divine life which is beyond both subject and object. Scientific knowledge is usually defined as knowledge of one or another object. But this is a definition which is adapted to the conditions of our objectivized world: it does not go deep enough. For in its depths, even the most positive, exactly scientific, knowledge of the natural world holds within itself a reflection of the Logos.

The old, traditional view recognizes an objective criterium of truth—Truth is almost made the equivalent of objectivity. This objectivism in the comprehension of truth and of true perception is peculiar not only to a so-called naïve realism which most philosophical tendencies refuse to accept: the idea still prevails of knowledge as conformity to "objective" reality, which is thus revealed. Kant's *Critique* breaks with this sort of objectivism and perceives the truth in the correspondence of reason with itself: truth is determined by one's attitude to the law of reason and by the concordance of ideas with each other. But even Kant holds to objectivism, to universal validity, related to transcendental consciousness. Kant's ideas of the subjective and the objective are contradictory and insufficiently elucidated. The Neokantism of the school of Windelband, Rickert and Laski, considers truth a value, but gives it a wrong interpretation in a spirit of non-creative normativism. Husserl inclines toward an objective idealism of consciousness, his own sort of Platonism torn away from the platonic myths. Only existential philosophy really breaks with the power of objectivism in either a realistic or an idealistic form, although existential philosophy follows various lines and sometimes turns into a new form of objectivation, as for instance with Heidegger as he frees himself from the old terminology. Truth in subjectivism and individualism is found only in Kirkegaard, but even here it lacks philosophical basis.

It must be said, first of all, that truth is not the conformity, in the knower, of reality objectively given. No one has ever explained how the reality of being may become the ideality of perception. When I say "this is a table," this is a sort of partial truth, but there is neither correspondence nor equivalence between that table and my statement that it is a table. This modest knowledge of "table" has pragmatic significance, first of all. There are degrees of perception of the truth, depending on the degree of community among people, and what they have in common with the world as a whole. But on the other hand, truth is not the agreement of reason with itself and its own universally valid laws. *The* truth, on which all partial truths must be made dependent, is not abstractly reasonable, but spiritual. But spirit lies beyond a rationalized opposition between subject and object. Truth does not mean staying within some closed ideas, in an inescapable circle of consciousness: truth is an unlocking —a revealing. Truth is not objective, but rather transsubjective. The height of perception is not egress by means of objectivation, but by transcending. The average, normal consciousness is adapted to the conditions of the objectivized world. And the logical universal validity of perception has sociological character. I have written before, that perception depends on the spiritual "commonality" of men. Truth is revealed to men possessing a high degree of spiritual commonality, truth that transcends the objective, or better the objectivized world. What we call "being" is not the final depth of value. Being is not the product of rational thought: It depends on the condition of consciousness and the condition of the world. Deeper than being is spiritual existence or spiritual life, which takes precedence over being. Integral truth is neither a reflection of, nor a correspondence with the reality of the world, but rather the triumph of the world's meaning. Meaning is not the triumph of logic, adapted to the world's fallen state and held down by the laws of logic, particularly the law of identity. The divine Logos triumphs over the meaninglessness of the objective world. Truth is the triumph of Spirit. Integral truth is God. And the rays from this complete, divine Truth of the Logos also fall on scientific, partial perception applied to a given, objective actuality of the world. The revelation of truth is a creative act of spirit, a human, creative act; a creative act which overcomes our slavery to the objective world. Perception is active, not passive. In reality phenomenology demands a passive knower: it considers activity a psychologism. This is why we must recognize that the phenomenology of Husserl is unfavourable to existential philosophy. Recognizing the active and creative nature of perception does not mean idealism, but rather the opposite.

The knowledge of truth is not a developing of rational concepts, but first of all an evaluation. Truth is the light of the Logos, lighted within being itself, if we use the traditional terminology, or in the depths of existence, or of life itself. This one complete Truth is divided into a multitude of truths. A sphere of knowledge lighted by one ray of light (such as a given science) may deny the source of light, the Logos-Sun. But it could never be lighted save for this one source of light. All knowers in various spheres of knowledge recognize logic and its laws which they

consider unchangeable. But they may deny the Logos,
the final integral spiritual Reason-Word. Now while the
laws of logic (the law of identity and the law of elimination of a *third*) necessarily means an adaptation to the
conditions of our fallen world, spirit is a sphere beyond
the laws of logic, but in Spirit is the light of the Logos.
I have frequently written of the sociological character of
the universality of logic and the relation of this universal
validity and conviction to the degree of spiritual commonality.

I do not wish to repeat what I have already said, but it
is specially important to make clear the following:
Neither materialism, nor phenomalism (in various types
of positivism), nor existentialism of Heidegger's type, can
give a basic argument for the very rise of the problem of
truth. In our day Heidegger is specially important. It is
quite incomprehensible how man (Dasein) can rise above
the baseness of the world, can escape from the realm of
"*das* Man". To make this possible there must be in
man a higher element which lifts him above the given
world. The existentialists of the anti-religious type think
so poorly of man, comprehend him so exclusively from
below, that it is incomprehensible how the problem of
knowledge, the glow of the light of Truth could ever
arise. No matter how we may think of man, we are
faced with the fact that he both knows the light of
truth, and is plunged into the darkness of mistakes and
error. Why is this tragedy possible? Why is it that the
light of the Logos does not always illumine man's percep-

tive path, since man is a spiritual being, surpassing the world? Knowledge is not an intellectual process only: in knowledge all of man's powers are engaged, voluntary choice, attraction to, and repulsion from, the truth. Descartes understood the dependence of errors on the will. The view of pragmatism, that truth is what is useful for life, is quite erroneous. Truth may be dangerous to everyday life. Christian truth might even become very dangerous—might cause the collapse of nations and civilizations. Hence pure Christian truth has been distorted and adapted to man's everyday life; the work of Christ has been corrected, as Dostoevsky's Grand Inquisitor says. But if we believe in the power of Truth unto salvation, this is in quite another sense: It is in relation to Truth that division is made between what is God's and what is Caesar's, between spirit and the world. At quite the other extreme, in the exact sciences of the world of nature, we are faced with the real tragedy of the scientist. Physics and Chemistry of the XXth century are making great discoveries, leading to stunning technical effects. But this success has led to the destruction of life, and a threat to the very existence of human civilization. Such is the work of dividing the atom and the invention of the atom bomb. Science, if it does not reveal the Truth, at least reveals truths, and our modern world is plunged ever deeper into shadow. Man is falling away from integral Truth and the separate truths he discovers do not help him. In a world falsely divided into two parts, a situation calling for extraordinary falsehood, scientific discoveries and technical inventions represent the terrible danger of more and more war. The chemists, perhaps quite unselfishly, discover at least partial truth, but the result has been the atomic bomb, which threatens our destruction. This goes on in the realm of Caesar. Salvation can come only by the light of integral Truth, which is revealed in the realm of Spirit.

\*
\*   \*

If we deny the so-called criteria of truth, in the sense of both naïve and rationalistic realism, as well as in the sense of transcendental-critical idealism, it is not at all in order to affirm an arbitrary "subjectivity", the "psychologism" in Husserl's use of the term, as over against a deep reality. Deep reality is revealed in subjectivity, which lies beyond objectivation. Truth is subjective and not objective: it becomes objectivized in relation to the world of necessity, the realm of Caesar, in the adaptation to the fractionization and sordid multiplicity of our world as it is. "Subjectivity" is the opposite of truth and deep reality: "subjectivity" closed within itself, incapable of transcendence, of getting out of itself: it is definition from without. Man is boxed up within  himself, an unfree being, determined not by depth, but from without, by the necessities of the world in which everything is torn apart, one part hostile to another;

nothing has depth, that is to say that nothing is spiritual. When the existentialists, Heidegger, Sartre and the others, talk of man's (Dasein) being cast out into the world and of man's being sentenced to this world, they are talking of an objectivation which makes man's fate inescapable, having lost the depth of reality. This can scarcely be disputed—it is an act of final, free election. I do not call this kind of philosophy existentialist, because it is captive to the power of the objective. The difference between this and the old classical ontological philosophy is this, that it encounters the objectivity of an absurd, meaningless world, while the earlier philosophy thought it was faced with the objectivity of reason and the true meaning of being. This is a very serious crisis of philosophical thought. But both these tendencies remain within the grip of objectivism.

Objectivation creates various worlds with greater or less degrees of reality or illusion. It is a mistake to think that all mankind lives in one and the same objective world, given from without. Man lives in various, sometimes fictitious worlds, which, if taken separately, do not correspond to complex and many-sided reality. And the quantity of fantasy and the phantasmagorical is determined by the degree to which each concentrates exclusively on one phase, excluding all the rest. Universalism in conceiving of the world is a very rare phenomenon. Men live in different worlds, the clergy and the theologians, scholars and inventors, politicians, social reformers and revolutionaries, writers and artists, men of action engrossed in their business—These people are often quite incapable of understanding each other. One's conception of the world also depends upon his beliefs and ideological tendencies: is he Catholic or Marxist, liberal or socialist, materialist or spiritualist, etc. Again, the world is viewed differently by different classes: capitalists, workers or intellectuals. More often than they think, men live in a realm of abstraction, fiction, myth. The most rational men live by myths. Rationalism itself is one of these myths. Rational abstraction is easily transformed into myth. Marxism, for instance, is full of abstractions which have become myths. Human consciousness is mobile: it contracts or expands, concentrates on some one point or is dissipated. The ideal of an average, normal consciousness is an abstraction. The reason of rationalism is a myth. The supposed heroism of fearless refusal of all belief in a higher, spiritual, divine world, refusal to accept any comfort, is also one of the myths of our time, one of the means of self-consolation.

Man is an unconsciously sly being, and never quite "normal"; he easily deceives both himself and others, most often himself. The construction of a personal world-concept, often illusory, depending on the thinker's tendencies, has a pragmatic quality which knowledge of true reality does not possess.

The Russian sociologists of the 1870's, who criticized naturalism in the social sciences, insisted on the subjective method in sociology and hence brought upon themselves the ridicule of the Marxists who,

although mistakenly, considered themselves objectivists
(N. Michailovsky and P. Lavrov). The class view-point is
also a subjective method in sociology. The Russian "sub-
jectivists" in sociology could not provide a philosophic
basis for their view-point, because they belonged to the
then prevailing positivist tendencies. But in the subjective
method in sociology, there was unquestionable truth.
More, even: the subjective method might be affirmed for
all of philosophy. Existential philosophy means using the
subjective method: it affirms the perception of the world
in human existence and true human existence: it is
anthropocentric. And protest against it by calling it
psychologism, is quite useless. Psychologism remains a
naturalistic tendency. There is more reason for calling it
ethicism, but this is also untrue. Ethicism is not a whole,
integral view-point, something spiritual which bases judgment in the depths of spirituality, which is revealed in
human existence. Spirit is something beyond the usual
disputes of subjectivism and objectivism. Evaluation is
the means of knowledge of the so-called science of the
spirit, but this evaluation reflects spirit rather than the
sphere of objectivation, which exists not alone in the
phenomena of nature, but in social and psychic phenomena as well. The historic world, or better the historic
worlds, which are known from the object, already have
to deal with objectivation. The true philosophy of history which is free from objectivation is messianic and
prophetic, that is, spiritual. In spiritual knowledge, pro-
foundly existentialist, Truth and Reason are revealed.

Objective knowledge knows only the realm of Caesar and not the realm of Spirit. Thus we face the sharp and final question: is there such a thing as genuine reality, not based on object, not illusory, not imaginary? Of course there is, but it is neither "objective" nor "subjective" in the wrong sense of the word: it lies beyond all secondary division into, and contrast between, subject and object: in Hindu terminology it is Atman and Brahma. Everything presupposes this reality, without which we are plunged into an illusory realm, into the factualness of objectivation, into the phantom power of objectivism, which is subjectivism as well, in the evil sense of this word. To a considerable degree we live in an illusory world of the "objective", created by a wrong tendency of the subject which has become enslaved to objective necessity. All religions have struggled against this enslavement and then, themselves, have set up a new captivity to objectivation. As a foundation of a philosophy which belongs to the realm of Spirit rather than to that of Caesar, there lies a spiritual religious experience, and not only that of Kirkegaard and Nietzsche, as Jaspers would have it. And in asserting this I would by no means deny the great importance of Kirkegaard and Nietzsche.

The existentialists of the new formation may say that my philosophical view-point presupposes the myth of God, the myth of the Spirit—let them call that a myth: this disturbs me not at all. This is the most universal and integral of all myths. What is most important is the myth concerning the existence of Truth, without which it is difficult to talk about the truth of anything, not only about Truth, but also about truths. The reality of the myth of God, of Spirit, of Truth, cannot be demonstrated, neither is this necessary. This is a matter of final choice, and presupposes freedom. I have good reason for considering myself an existentialist, although to a greater degree I could call mine the philosophy of the spirit, and still more an eschatological philosophy. But here is where I differ radically from the existentialists of to-day: they consider man's worth to be in the fearless acceptance of death, as the final truth. Man lives in order to die: his life is life for death. Even Freud considered the instinct of death the most noble in man, of whom, by the way, he had a very low opinion. Essentially, Heidegger sees in death the sole triumph over the baseness of "*das* Man," i.e. sees in death a greater depth of value, than in life. Man is a finite being: infinity is not revealed in him, and death belongs to his nature. Sartre and Simon de Beauvoir are willing to see in death a positive value. I consider this modern tendency a defeat of Spirit, decadence, the idolatry of death. Unquestionably, man's dignity is revealed in his fearlessness before death, in his free acceptance of death in this world, but only for the sake of a final victory over death, for struggle against death's triumph. All religions have fought against death. Christianity is first of all a religion of resurrection. Against this modern tendency to recognize the triumph of death as the last word in life, we should place the very Russian thought of N. Fedoroff, the great fighter against death, who recognized not only the idea of resurrection, but actual raising from the dead. The existentialists are above the Marxists, because after all they recognize the problem, which for the Marxists does not exist. For the marxists submersion in the collectivity and activity in it wipes out the very question of death. But with all the pitifulness of this solution, they at least do not deify death. If there is not a resurrection of all who have lived into eternal life, if there is no immortality, then the world is absurd and meaningless. The existentialists of to-day do not see this absurdity and meaninglessness. Sartre seeks a way out in the recognition of man's freedom, which is not determined by his nature. Man, according to Sartre, is a low type of being, but by means of his freedom he may make himself and his world better. This should have brought Sartre to a recognition of the ideal, spiritual element in man. Without this, existentialists are bound to fall into materialism, even if it be a refined materialism. We might compare the ideas of Sartre, Camus and others with the tragic humanism of Herzen, for whom the world was accidental and meaningless, but man a free being who could create a better world. But Herzen, like Nietzsche later, knew religious torment, something not evident in to-day's existentialists. Deeper truth lies in the fact that the world is not meaningless and absurd, but is in a meaningless state. This world, the world as it appears to us, is a fallen world: in it death, absurd and meaningless, triumphs. Another world, that of reason and freedom, is revealed only in spiritual experience, something

modern existentialists deny. We must view the meaningless and absurd world in which we live, but at the same
time believe in spirit, which includes freedom, and in
reason, which overcomes meaninglessness and transforms
the world. This will be the triumph of the realm of Spirit
over that of Caesar; the triumph of Truth, not only over
falsehood, but over all the partial, fractional truths which
have claimed to be of cardinal importance.

There is nothing higher than the search for, and the
love of Truth. Truth, the one integral truth, is God, and
to perceive Truth is to enter divine life. Substitution for
the one integral, liberating truth by small, partial truths
which pretend to be universal, leads to idolatry and
slavery. On this basis arises scientism, something which is
not at all science. All partial truths involve relationship,
although not always realized, with one supreme Truth.
Knowledge of the Truth cannot be human knowledge
alone, but neither can it be only divine knowledge, as for
instance in Hegel's monistic idealism; it can only be
divine-human knowledge. Knowledge of Truth is creative
activity of man, who bears the image and likeness of God,
i.e. contains within himself a divine element. This element is the Divine "otherness". The knowledge of the
Truth toward which science strives, is impossible by
means of abstract reason, operating with concepts: it is
possible only by means of a spiritually integral reason,
by spirit and spiritual experience. Western European
thought struggles in the contrast between rationalism
and irrationaiism, both of which are the result of the

fractionalization of the spiritual world. Existential philosophy, as well, is stopped by this fact. This is specially
evident in Jaspers. They arrive at this: philosophical
knowledge should be existential, but this is impossible
because the perceiving reason cannot know something
which can never be object. But knowledge of being
outside objectivation is possible, and has always been
known by the elite, even in ancient India. Spiritual
knowing is divine-human, knowledge neither by reason
nor by feeling, but by integral Spirit. Denial of divine-
human knowledge of Truth leads to substituting for
Truth, self-interest and the will to power. Knowledge of
Truth means the transfiguration, the enlightenment of
the world and not abstract knowledge; in such knowledge theory and practice coincide. There is in man an
active, creative element, to which knowledge is related.
This active element is spiritual. In knowledge there is a
Theurgical element, giving man the capacity to satisfy
not only the realm of Caesar, but that of the Spirit. When,
in the past, philosophers talked of innate ideas, because
of the static nature of their thinking, they expressed per-
fectly the truth of the active spirit in man and in human
knowledge. Unless we admit this activity of spirit within
man, we can understand nothing about him, we cannot
even admit that he is possible. It is astonishing that
man is not so overwhelmed by the evil infinity of the
world, that he is deprived of the possibility of knowing
Truth. Neither judgment nor reason could ever reveal
the possibility of knowing truth: only the spirit does

this. In Greek "NOUS" is not only reason, but spirit as well. Spirit is not something opposite to the rational or the irrational. The true existentialist philosophy is philosophy of the spirit.

Modern philosophy is inclined to deny the dualism of the world, the noumenal and the phenomenal, which we derive from Plato. This is nothing new: we find it in phenomenalism, empirism, positivism, in immanent monism, in materialism. The same tendency is found in Nietzsche, in the modern existentialists and many others. Only at present this is taking on more refined forms. I think that here we have a basic contrast between two types of philosophy: those which are satisfied with the given world, and those which transcend it. But what does the dualism of the world mean, and how are we to reconcile this with scientific perception? First of all, we must eliminate ontological dualism and all use of static concepts of substance. This does not mean the dualism of spirit and body, of spirit and material, which we find in academic spiritualistic tendencies. This is a question of two *conditions* of the world, corresponding to two different structures and ways of knowing, above all the dualism of freedom and necessity; inner unity and disunity and hostility, meaning and the lack of it. We live in a world of necessity, of disunity and hostility, of the absurd and meaningless. But the world does not begin and end with this condition, which is actually our fallen state: another condition of the world is possible and it requires another type of knowing. Further, there is no basis for asserting

that only one world exists. It is all-important to recognize
that spirit is not a reality comparable with other realities,
like material, for example: spirit is reality in quite another
sense. It is freedom and not being: it is a qualitative
changing of the data of the world, it is creative energy
which transfigures the world. Further, there is no spirit
without God, as its original source. Man's spiritual experience, on which alone metaphysics can be based, is the
only proof of the existence of God. The world of necessity,
estrangement and hostility, of the absurd and final, is a
world of limited, surface consciousness, to which infinity
is inaccessible. There are other planes of the life of the
world which may be revealed only to an altered consciousness. In this the occultists are right: the world, the
one world of God, is one of many planes. But how can we
reconcile with this the possibility of scientific perception?
This does not in the least cause difficulty for science in the
exact meaning of the word, and it calls forth no conflict.
Science knows the real world in its present state, and
science is not responsible for the fact that ours is a fallen
world. Science seeks truth: in it the Logos is reflected.
But it has definite limits, and there are questions which
it not only cannot solve, but may not even put. The conflict arises from science's pretension to the highest place
in human life, its claimed ability to solve authoritatively
questions of religion, philosophy, morals, to give directives for the creativeness of spiritual culture. This really
brings conflict. But neither exact science, nor science of
any kind, has anything to say as to whether or not

other worlds exist. If science denies the existence of
other worlds, it is only because the scientist is plunged
completely into this our given world and does not possess
that freedom of the spirit which is necessary for recognizing other planes of the world. Scientism preaches
slavery to the world. It must be said that orthodox
theology, also, considers it necessary to deny the existence of many planes of the world and also preaches
enslavement to the world. Origen's doctrine of many
worlds was condemned, and for the same reason. Thus
partial truth claims to be the one Truth, which is
revealed only to a consciousness which is constantly
deepened and widened, that is to consciousness growing
in the spiritual. Our given world is a partial world, as
a day of our life is partial and incomplete.

# CHAPTER I

# MAN AND GOD—SPIRITUALITY

Man faces that question of all questions, the question of God. This question is rarely put in its pure and original state: it has become too attached to a scholasticism which stultifies, to verbal philosophy, to the play of concepts. The very persons who have tried to lift up the idea of God have terribly degraded it, imputing to God qualities taken from the realm of Caesar, not from the realm of Spirit. There is no guarantee of God's existence: man can always doubt and deny. God does not force us to recognize Him, as do material objects; He appeals to man's freedom. Belief in God is only an internal meeting with Him in spiritual experience. We must recognize conclusively that all of the traditional proofs of the existence of God, ontological, cosmological, or physico-theological, are not only insolvent: they are quite unnecessary, even harmful. Kant's criticism of these proofs of God's existence is very convincing, and has not been overthrown by traditional apologetics. What might be called the anthropological proof is much stronger. It consists in the fact that man is a being belonging to two worlds, and for this reason he is not included completely in this world of necessity: he transcends himself as a being of the empiric, revealing a freedom which does not derive from this world. This does not prove, but it does show, the existence of God, since it reveals the spiritual element in man. Still more important is primal feeling, which cannot be fully expressed. Try for a minute to imagine a self-sufficient world, for example, the self-sufficiency of moving material, viewed as the essential base and cause, and you will be astonished at the incomprehensibility, the meaninglessness, the darkness and unrealizability of the idea of such a world. The indubitable result of meditation about God is this: it is impossible to think of God in rational terms, which are always borrowed from this world, which is not at all like God. Only apophatic theology was right: you cannot construct an ontology of God. God is not being, which is always a development of abstract thought. God is not being, God is Spirit. God is not essence, but existence. About God we can speak only in the symbolic language of spiritual experience. In general, metaphysics is possible only as a symbolic of spiritual experience, or an intuitive description of spiritual contacts. Neither can we put the question of God apart from man. Taken in its depth, and not superficially, the existence of man is the only witness to the existence of God, since man is the reflection of God's image, although he so often deforms it. Man is not only a finite being, as modern thought would affirm; he is also an infinite being: he is infinity in a finite form, a synthesis of the finite and the infinite. Man's dissatisfaction with the finite, his longing for the infinite reveals the divine in man, it is the human testimony to the existence of God, and not merely of the world. The concept of

God as a self-sufficient and immovable being is a limited and abstract rational idea: such a concept is not given in spiritual experience where the relationships with God are always dramatic. Men meet God not in being, about which they think in concepts, but rather in spirit, in spiritual experience. In being there is already either objectivation, or a deadly abstraction of concepts, or else an idealized natural necessity and social compulsion. Only a meeting in spirit is a meeting in freedom. Only in spirit and in freedom, the meeting with God is a dramatic event.

\*
\* \*

The relationship between man and God is paradoxical and cannot at all be expressed in concepts. God is born in man, and because of this man is lifted up and enriched. This is one side of divine-human truth: it is revealed in man's experience. But there is another side, less clearly revealed. Man is born in God, and by this the divine life is enriched. Man needs God, and God needs man. This presupposes man's creative reply to God. The relationship between God and man may be understood only dramatically, i.e. dynamically. We cannot conceive of God, statically: a static conception is rational and exoteric. The symbolism of the Bible is dramatic and dynamic in the highest degree. Static ontology is taken from Greek philosophy. Admitting the existence of two natures, divine and human, which may be united, but are not identical and not fused, is a truth incomprehensible to the objectivizing reason—it is supra-rational, since reason itself inclines either to monism or to dualism. The secret of Christianity which is presented rationally in theological systems, is bound up with this paradoxical and dramatic relationship between the divine and the human. The paradox lies in this, that supreme humanity is divine; an expression of man and of humanity at the same time. This presents reason with a contradiction which is rationally insoluble. One might say that while God is human, man is non-human. Hence in reality only God-human humanity can exist. The basic problem is not that of God, but rather that of God-man and divine-humanity. The assertion of God outside divine-humanity, that is, abstract monotheism, is a form of idolatry. Hence the tremendous importance of the doctrine of the Trinity, which must be understood mystically, in the terms of spiritual experience, and not by rational theology. The great German mystics, especially Eckhardt and Angelius Silesius, said that there is no God without man, that God disappears when man disappears. This must be understood spiritually, and not in the terms of naturalistic metaphysics and naturalistic theology. This is an experience of love, rather than of understanding. For us the basic contrast should be not a scholastic contrast of the natural with the supernatural, which was unknown to the Greek Fathers of the Church, but a contrast between the natural and the spiritual. There are two ways of understanding the trans-

cendental: God may be conceived as transcending my
limitations, as mystical, actual infinity, which assumes
the existence of a divine element in man himself—or as
an ontological reality outside man which presupposes the
alienation of human nature, places it outside divinity.
Only the former concept is spiritual and not idolatrous.
The idea so often expressed that before God man is
nothing, is quite false and degrading. On the contrary,
we must affirm that before God, and turned toward God,
man is lifted and ennobled, he conquers nothingness. The
rational ontological doctrines concerning the relationship
between God and man are inadmissible—such have only
pedagogical and social meaning for Christian societies.
Even more must we reject the view, widespread in theological teaching, that God is the cause of the world, the
first cause. Now causality and causal relationships are
completely inapplicable to the relationship between God
and the world, between God and man. Causality is a
category applicable only to the world of phenomena,
not at all applicable to the noumenal world. Kant expressed this clearly, though he was inconsistent when he
recognized a causal relationship between the thing-in-
itself, and its appearance. God is not the cause of the
world. We may say that God is the foundation of the
world, its creator, but even these are imperfect words. We
must free ourselves of all sociomorphism and cosmo-
morphism. God is not a force in the natural sense of the
word, acting in space and time. He is not the master and
director of the world. He is neither the world itself, nor

the force released in the world. It is more correct to say that God is the Meaning, the Truth of the world. God is Spirit and Freedom. If, in contrast with pantheistic to monism, we say that God is a person, this must be understood, not in the limited natural-human sense, but in the spiritual sense of a concrete image, with which personal contact is possible for us. Contact and relationship with God is possible, not as relationship with the Absolute, for whom there can be no other, with whom there can be no relationship, not with the God of apophatic theology, but with a real, personal God who has relationship to others. A world without God is an impossible contradiction of the finite with the infinite, accidental and void of meaning.

Man cannot be self-sufficient: that would mean that he did not exist. In this lies the secret of human existence: it proves the existence of something higher than man and in this is man's own worth. Man is a being who overcomes his limitations, transcends to something higher. If there is no God, as Truth and Meaning, if there is no higher Justice, then everything flattens out, and there is neither any one nor any thing to which man can rise. If, on the other hand, man is God, the situation is flatter still, hopeless and worthless. Every qualitative value is an indication that in the path of man's life there lies something higher than man. And that which is higher than man, i.e. the divine, is not an exterior force standing above and ruling him, but that which, in him, makes him truly man —his higher freedom. Here the difference between trans-

cendent and immanent terminology is conditional, and
only shows the inescapable paradox in the conditions of
our times. At the dawn of his existence, man presupposed
the existence of divinity, although in very rude forms. If
there is no God, no Justice higher than this world, then
man is completely subject to necessity or to nature, to the
cosmos or to society, to the state. Man's freedom lies in
this, that beside the realm of Caesar there is also the
realm of Spirit. The existence of God is revealed in the
existence of spirit in man. And God resembles neither
the forces of nature, nor the authority of society or of the
state. Here no analogy is valid: all analogy would mean
slavish cosmo-morphism and sociomorphism in the understanding of God. God is freedom, and not necessity, not
authority over man and the world. What the theologians
call grace, placing it alongside human freedom, is this
action in man of divine freedom. We might say that the
existence of God is man's charter of liberty, his inner
justification for his struggle for freedom against nature
and society. Man's worth consists in his not submitting to
something lower than himself. But for this to be possible,
there must be something higher than himself, even
though not outside or above him. The error of humanism
was not in its assertion of the supreme value of man and
his creative calling, but rather in its tendency to consider
man self-sufficient, and hence to have too low an idea of
him. Considering man as an exclusively natural being,
humanism did not perceive in him the spiritual being.
Christ taught that man is the image and likeness of God,

and by that the worth of man, as a free spiritual being, was confirmed: man was not a slave to natural necessity. Freedom is possible only if, beside the realm of Caesar, there exists the realm of Spirit, that is, the Kingdom of God. I repeat. God is not an objective being, to whom rational concepts are applicable: God is Spirit. The basic quality of Spirit is Freedom. Spirit is not nature. Freedom cannot be rooted in nature, but in Spirit. Man's connection with God is not of the nature of natural being, but spiritual-existential, of the depths. If there is no God, there is no Mystery, and if there is no Mystery, then the world is flat and man is a two-dimension being, incapable of rising higher. If there is no God, there is no victory over death, no eternal life: everything is meaningless and absurd. God is completeness toward which man cannot avoid striving. The existence of man does not prove the existence of God by lifeless, logical dialectic, but rather indicates God's existence, bears witness to Him. To identify the realm of Spirit with the realm of Caesar, in one or another form, is a false monism, which inevitably gives rise to slavery. Dualism between the realm of spirit and that of Caesar is an absolutely necessary confirmation of man's freedom. But this is not a final dualism: it is dualism in the spiritual and religious life of man. The final monism will be confirmed in the Kingdom of God: it is only revealed eschatologically.

*

*    *

The mystical doctrine of Providence, considering God to be the Lord and Director of this world, must disturb not only the most refined consciousness, but that less developed, or even little developed. How are we to connect this doctrine with the triumph of evil and suffering in our world? I think this is one of the chief sources of atheism. The usual way out of this difficulty is by means of the doctrine of the Fall of man. But this neither explains nor justifies anything. The power of evil remains unexplained. Men's suffering is disproportionate to their sinfulness. It is not the worse, but the better people, who suffer most. Unexplained also are the periods, both individual and historical, when a man feels that he has been deserted by God. Explaining terrible catastrophies in human life as God's anger and punishment is insufferable. It is terribly difficult to explain and justify the omnipresence of an all-powerful and all-beneficent God in evil, in plague and cholera, in torture-chambers, in the horrors of war, of revolution and counter-revolution. Our concept of the action of divine Providence in this world of evil and suffering needs to be revaluated. Kirkegaard is considerably nearer the truth when he says that God remains in this world incognito. This world is controlled not by God, but by the prince of this world, with his laws, laws of the world and not of God. This world is subject more to the realm of Caesar than to the realm of Spirit. God's response can be comprehended only eschatologically: "Thy Kingdom come": it is not yet here. The world of objects and phenomena, with the necessity reigning in it, is only an outer sphere, but beyond it there is hidden a depth of relationship to God. We cannot think that God causes things in this world in the same way as do the forces of nature, that He directs and rules as do kings and other authorities in a state, that He determines the life of the world and of men. We cannot think of progress in relation to God, within the progress of history, of historic necessity. In history we have the conflict of freedom with necessity: but God may exist only in freedom; He is not present in necessity. This leads us to a complete change in the doctrine about Providence. Grace is not a power acting from without: grace is the revelation of the divine in man. There is no conflict between grace and freedom: grace is only transfigured freedom.

As I have frequently said, making it my basic theme, we may contrast grace with evil and the material, with pre-existent and uncreated freedom, and hence freedom as-yet-undefined and irrational. But freedom may become transfiguration. Hence in the history of man and the world irrational forces or an obscure freedom may operate, giving rise to necessity and violence. But transfigured freedom, too, can act—divine power is also active. Therefore history is dramatic in the extreme: therefore there is in history a constant collision and struggle between the realm of Spirit and that of Caesar, which tends to become totalitarian. It is wrong, however, to see everywhere in the life of the world the triumph of evil, diabolic forces, and equally wrong to see the progressive revelation and triumph of divine, good forces. Spirit is not revealed progressively in the historic process; it is the evidently evil which triumphs, but we must perceive, everywhere, possible new conceptions and the inflowing of the spirit and the spiritual realm. Man's relation to God presupposes a dramatic struggle between the realm of Spirit and that of Caesar, passing through dualism, but for the sake of a final monism which can be revealed only eschatologically. And all this is complicated by man's relation to the cosmos.

# CHAPTER II

# MAN AND THE COSMOS—TECHNICS

MAN IS A NATURAL being: he is bound by many threads to the life of the cosmos; he is dependent on the cycle of cosmic life. Man's body, even, is determined by physics and by chemical processes. He dies, and his physical body is dissolved into the matter and the life of the world. Man lives in a world of nature and has to define his relationship to it. But the mystery of man is that he is not only a natural being, explicable by nature; he is also a personality, that is a spiritual being, bearing in himself the divine image. Hence the tragedy of man's situation in the natural world. Man is not only one of the objects of this world; above all he is subject, not derivable from the object. At the same time, man's relation to the cosmos is defined by the fact that he is a microcosm: he includes within himself the cosmos, or he includes within himself history. Man cannot be only a part of something: he is a whole. Because of the spiritual element in him, man is not subject to nature: he is independent, although natural forces may kill him. If man were only a natural and finite being, there would be nothing tragic about death—only the death is tragic of a deathless being, striving toward infinity. Man is part of nature only from without, from the object: From within, from spirit, nature is in him. Hence man's double relation to the cosmos: he is the slave of nature, and nature's king. Man's central position in the cosmos is not determined by astronomy, and has not changed since Copernicus: it is not at all dependent on the discoveries of the natural sciences. This central position of man is determined by spirit, hence our basic theme—spirit and nature, freedom and necessity.

We may fix four periods in man's relationship to the cosmos: 1. man's submersion in cosmic life, his dependence on the objective world—human personality has not yet been fully developed—man has not yet conquered nature: his relation toward nature is still in terms of magic and myth (primitive stock-raising and agriculture, slavery); 2. Man is freed from the power of cosmic forces, from the spirits and demons of nature—man struggles by means of ascesis, rather than technics (elementary forms of economics, serfdom); 3. the mechanization of nature, its scientific and technical control, the development of industry in the form of capitalism, the emancipation of labour and its enslavement by exploitation of the means of production, the necessity of selling labour for wages, and 4. the disruption of cosmic order in the discovery of the infinitely great and the infinitely small, the formation of a new organization, distinct from the organic, technics and mechanization, the terribly augmented power of man over nature, and his slavery to his own discoveries. These phases in the relationships between man and nature are typological and not chronological, although the passage of time plays a certain part. But now, when we have entered the technical age, other terrible themes present themselves. Where once man feared the demons of nature and Christ freed him from demonolatry, now man is in terror before the world-wide mechanization of nature. The power of technics is the final metamorphosis of the realm of Caesar. It no longer demands the sanctification which the realm of Caesar demanded, in the past. This is the last phase of secularization, the dissolution of the centre and the development of various autonomous spheres, where one of them claims totalitarian recognition. Man is now in the grip of one of these autonomous spheres. We may conceive of a fifth period in the relationship between man and nature. In this period will come man's still greater control of the forces of nature, the real emancipation of labour and the workers, technics made subject to spirit. But this requires a spiritual movement in the world, which is the work of freedom.

I have often said that the unbelievable power of technics has revolutionized the whole of human life. The crisis through which we are living is due to the lack of balance between man's spiritual and physical organization on the one hand, and modern technics, on the other; Man's body and mind were formed at a time when human life was still in rhythm with the rhythm of nature, when for him cosmic order still existed. Man was still bound to Mother-earth. The power of technics means the end of this tellurgic epoch. The organic, natural surroundings of man, earth, vegetation, animal life, etc., may be destroyed by technics, but what then? In primitive times an elementary technics existed: then toward the end of the

XVIIIth century the machine broke in with revolutionary power, and with it came the development of capitalist industry. It is only in our time that technics acquires a determining influence on man and human society; only now a type of technical civilization is emerging. This cannot be said of the XIXth century, which was complex and contradictory, but still retained the old type of culture. Now the bases have been shaken of that cosmic order in which both the positivists and the materialists of the XIXth century believed. Man is faced with cosmic forces in a new way. The cosmos, in the antique Greek sense, the cosmos of Aristotle, of Dante and Thomas Aquinas, no longer exists. Nature is no longer a hierarchic order, established by God, and on which man may depend. This change began with Copernicus. Pascal, already, felt terror in the face of limitless space, and was acutely conscious of man's being lost in a strange, cold, infinite universe. But our terror should be no less great as we face the revelation of the ultra-microscopic universe. Science has entered the interior structure of nature, the very depths of material. In this connection the work on dissolving the atom is of the greatest significance. It has led to the development of the atomic bomb, which threatens unheard-of disaster. It frightens the scientists, who no longer feel themselves free in their laboratories. The fission of material releases gigantic energy. It may be said that material had bound and imprisoned energy. This stabilized the cosmic order. Now the scientists tell us that their discoveries, with their technical consequences, may explode the cosmic order, call forth cosmic catastrophes. War has ceased to be a localized phenomenon, something between nations and states—it has become something cosmic, or rather anti-cosmic.

Another element of great importance in changing our views of cosmic order was the discovery of the laws of relativity. This put an end to the evolutionary optimism of the XIXth century, with its conviction that everything is moving for the best in the world of nature. The evolutionary theories grew out of the biological sciences, and had a limited horizon: Now it is physics and chemistry which dominate, and the horizon becomes as wide as the cosmos, and this at the very moment when the cosmos itself is almost shattered. Our attitude toward nature is determined solely by experimentation and the possibilities of experiment are limitless. This may give rise either to optimism or to pessimism.

\*

\*    \*

A new reality is appearing, different from both the realities of inorganic and of organic nature. This is an organized reality. Man no longer has to deal with a nature created by God, but with a new reality made by man and by civilization, a reality of machines and technics which do not exist in nature. Machines are made from material elements taken from the old nature, but into them goes something quite new, no longer of nature, and not a part of the old cosmic order. Man did not at first see what results might come from this. Truly, machines and technics have a cosmogonic significance. This is a new day of creation—or a new night. Probably night, for the light of the sun may be darkened. But technics has a double role: it has both positive and negative significance. And the romantic refusal to accept technics is powerless and reactionary. We should not deny the scientific discoveries of technics, but rather learn their spiritual control.

One of the fateful results of technics subject only to its own laws, which have produced world wars, is the exaggerated development of etatism. The state becomes omnipotent. Etatism is increasing, not only in the totalitarian states; it refuses to recognize any limits to its power, and considers man only as its instrument, its means to an end. Another result of the power of technics, for which man is insufficiently adapted, and which causes him great difficulty, is the terrible shortening of time, a speed with which man cannot keep pace. No single moment is of value in itself—it is only a means for the next. Incredible activity is demanded of man, giving him no time to recover his balance. But these active minutes make man passive. He becomes a means outside the human process; he is only a function of the process of production. The activity of man's spirit is weakened. Man is valued in utilitarian terms, according to his productivity. This means an estrangement of man's nature—

really the destruction of man. Marx spoke truly of the estrangement of man's nature in the degenerating process of the capitalist system. But the same estrangement is continued in the system which Marx would substitute for capitalism. In the technical epoch, also, we have great masses of people entering the process of history—just at the moment when they have lost their religious beliefs. These masses should not be identified with the labouring-classes. All this has brought us to a grave crisis of man and of human civilization: What is the chief cause of this crisis?

Since he moved out of the Middle Ages, man has followed a path marked by the autonomy of different spheres of creative activity. In the period of modern history, which has already ceased to be modern and has become very old, all spheres of culture and of social life began to live and develop by their own laws, independent of any spiritual centre. Hence some of the creative powers, held captive in the Middle Ages, could develop—Politics, economics, science, technics, nationality, etc.—none of these will recognize any moral law, any spiritual element higher than themselves. Machiavellism in politics, capitalism in economics, scientism in science, nationalism in the life of peoples, the integral power of technics over man—all these are the results of those autonomies. The basic and fatal contradiction in the fate of European man was that the autonomy of various spheres of his activity was not the autonomy of man himself, as an integral being. Man became more and more the slave of these autonomous spheres of activity, which were not under subjection to the human spirit. This increasing loss of man's integrity gives rise in him to the need to save himself from the threatening destruction, from the loss of his human image. Hence European man moves toward neo-humanism on the one hand, and on the other tries to regain integrality in the totalitarian organization of his whole life.

The problem of totalitarism, of which so much has been written, is more complex than is ordinarily thought. Totalitarism is a religious tragedy: in it is revealed man's religious instinct, his need for an integral relation to life. But the autonomy of various spheres of human activity, the loss of a spiritual centre, have led to a situation where the partial, the divided, claim totalitarity, integrality. Science and politics long ago began to present such claims. In our day, economics, technics, war have become totalitarian. In regard to these spheres, science takes on a utilitarian aspect. Marxism strives for man's integrality, will not be reconciled with the estrangement of human nature which occurs in the capitalist epoch. But Marx tries to create an integral man out of the divided, autonomous sphere of economics. He himself is caught by the power of economics of the capitalist epoch. For this reason Marxist totalitarism is false: instead of liberating man, it enslaves him. In the depths of his being man is not primarily a creature of economics.

But most important are the totalitarian claims of technics. Technics refuses to recognize anything higher than itself. It is forced, however, to reckon with the state, which, in its turn, takes on more and more of the totalitarian. The astounding development of technics as an autonomous sphere has led to the most basic phenomenon of our epoch: to transition from organic life to organized life. In our technical epoch, the life of great masses of men demanding a solution to the problem of their daily bread, has to be organized and regulated. Man is divorced from nature in the old sense of this word, and submerged in the closed social world as we see it in Marxism. And at the same time, man is acquiring a more and more planetary sense of the earth. Man's life is besieged by contradictions, he has lost his sense of balance. The autonomous authority of technics is the final expression of the realm of Caesar, a new form, unlike anything before it. The dualism of the realm of Spirit and that of Caesar is taking on ever more acute forms. The realm of Caesar refuses to recognize any neutral sphere: it thinks in monistic terms.

Our epoch is characterized by the union of rational and irrational. This may seem contradictory, but in reality it is understandable. There is an explosion of irrational forces, and man sinks in the resultant chaos. He tries to escape destruction by means of rationalization. But rationalization is only the reverse side of the irrational. Man's situation in the world becomes absurd and meaningless. Lost in the meaninglessness of life, he fails to recognize the only meaning which can justify this meaninglessness. The world is moving into rationalized

darkness. Even the rationalization of life may be irrational, for rationalization itself takes place at the very
moment when faith and reason totter. This makes the
whole process of life contradictory. The domination of
rationalized technics makes man's position in the world
absurd. This situation, man's exile into a world of the
absurd, is reflected in the philosophy of Heidegger and
the novels of Kafka. Here, the problem of man is put
with a new acuteness, and the demand for a new religious
and philosophical anthropology. The technicalization of
life means life's de-humanization. The old humanism
is powerless before the huge process of technics, before
the increasing consciousness of life's absurdity. Only the
Marxists try to remain optimistic: they believe that technics are a good thing, claiming that the apparent
absurdity of life is due only to the bourgeoisie, already
doomed to destruction, which will bring on the inevitable triumph of the proletariat. This view-point considers man as only a social being, in which class thinks
and creates. Marxist optimism does not consider deeply
enough the problem of man's relation to the cosmos,
or that of man's spiritual life, which is simply denied.
I have spoken, earlier, of humanism's dualism, its
internal dialectic, which leads to a denial of man, himself. There is no point in trying to deny technics. Technics should not be denied, it should rather be made
subject to spirit. In his historic progress, man's fate passes
through not only radical changes in social life, changes
which must create a new social structure, but also

through radical changes in his relationship with cosmic life. It is too often forgotten that human social life is closely tied to cosmic life, and that the perfect society cannot be attained without taking into consideration the life of the cosmos, and the action of cosmic forces. The bases of marxism are indefensible in the social world: the development of technics and its power over human life is directly related to the question, "Man and the cosmos." As has already been said, man's spiritual and moral development has not kept pace with his technical development, and this is the chief reason for his loss of equilibrium. Only a movement which combines the social and the spiritual can lead man out of this divided and lost condition. Only by means of the spiritual element, which is man's relationship to God, can man become independent and free himself from the necessity of nature and the power of technics. But spiritual development in man does not mean his turning away from nature and technics; it means rather his full command over them. The problem man has to face is even more complex: there can be no mutual relationship between him and mechanized nature. The communion between man and nature which existed in earlier times, is now possible only by spiritual vision: it cannot be simply organic in the old sense of that word. Still more acute is the problem of man's relationship to society.

# CHAPTER III

# MAN AND SOCIETY—SOCIALISM

MAN IS AT ONCE a natural, a social, and a spiritual being. He is also a being both free and slave, inclined both to sacrifice and love, and to egoism: he is both high and low; he bears in himself the image of God and the image of the world, of the natural and the social. Hence man is determined by his relations toward God, toward nature and toward society. He sometimes feels his relation to society far more keenly than his relation to the cosmos, and still more strongly feels the power of society over him. He senses the power of technics as the power of society, rather than that of nature. Hence the increased acuteness of the problem of the limits of society's power over man. Society has totalitarian pretensions and is inclined to say to man: "You are my creation and you belong entirely to me." Christ asserted a dualism: the Kingdom of God and that of Caesar. We are now living through a period of return to the ancient, heathen consciousness, which recognized the complete authority of the state and of society. Now the relations between man and society seem paradoxical. Considered from without, as object, human personality is only a small part of society. Considered from within, as subject, society is part of human personality, its social side, just as the cosmos is part of human personality seen as microcosm which includes everything in itself. It is most important to recognize that man belongs not only to the social plane, but to the spiritual plane as well, and that this is the source of his freedom. With all our power we should unmask the falsehood inherent in every monism, always a source of tyranny. Conceived monistically, society always has tyrannical tendencies. Pluralism would be more acceptable, but pluralism in bourgeois and capitalist societies is bound up with individualism and is a disguised form of tyranny by means of capitalist control. Hence we find acceptable only the idea of creating a quite new brotherly society, personalist and *communautaire*. For man society is an object, determining him from without. He must transform it into subject which, from within, will determine his own communal and social character.

Like Fascism, Communism denies the tragic conflict of personality with society. This conflict is held to be characteristic only of a society made up of different classes. Considered superficially, this may appear true, but in the depths of reality this conflict can be resolved only in the Kingdom of God. The tragedy of man's position lies in the fact that he is obliged to live in both natural and objectivized orders, that is, the influence of necessity upon him is greater than that of freedom. Society is neither a distinct being nor an organism. In this connection, the metaphysics of collectivism, which consider the social collective as something of higher value than man, is quite wrong. We shall return to this question later. But society is still a certain reality: a reality not only of "I" and "thou", but of "we". But this reality "we" by no means gives us the right to recognize the precedence of society over human personality. Outside man, beyond the relation of man to man, society does not exist, or else it exists as the alienation, exteriorally, of man's real nature. The universalism of Hegel, Marx, Durkheim, Spann and others, recognizing the precedence of society or the state over human personality, is a false universalism, based on the logic of a realism of concepts, in which the general is more real than the individual. In this connection Marx is contradictory, but in this contradiction to materialism there is a scholastic realism of concepts. For Marx, class is more real than man. It is very interesting that this contradiction of social dialectic, as J.-J. Rousseau asserted, leads to the despotic state of the Jacobins. Rousseau had already denied freedom of religious conscience, and had returned to the antique pre-Christian concept of freedom. Proudhon, and in Russia Herzen and N. Michailovsky, were nearer the truth in asserting socialism for the sake of the individual, for the sake of man.

*
* *

Freedom of the human personality cannot be given by society, and by its source and nature it cannot depend upon society—it belongs to man himself, as a spiritual being. And society, unless it makes totalitarian claims, can only recognize this freedom. This basic truth about freedom was reflected in the doctrines of natural law, of the rights of man, independent of the state, of freedom, not only as freedom within society, but freedom from society with its limitless claims on man. Benjamin Constant noted this in the difference between the concept of freedom in the Christian period of history and that in the ancient Greco-Roman world. The doctrine of natural law, recognizing the rights of man, independent of political rights fixed by the state, made a theoretical mistake characteristic of the immature metaphysic of that time. In reality, the inalienable rights of man, which fix the limits of society's authority over him, are fixed not by nature, but by spirit. They are spiritual rather than natural rights: nature establishes no rights whatever. The mistake occurred when they made a revolution in the name of nature; revolution may be made only in the name of spirit: nature, that is the natural instinct in man, created only new forms of slavery. Once Christianity made a supreme spiritual revolution: it made man spiritually free of the unlimited power of society and the state, which in the antique world included religious life as well. Christianity disclosed a spiritual element in man which depended not on the world or nature or society, but only on God. This is the truth in Christian personalism, unknown to the pre-Christian world. But in the course of history Christianity was deformed by its adaptation to the realm of Caesar; it bowed before the authority of the state, and undertook to sanctify this authority. In this way the compulsory Christian theocracies were formed, in this way men arrived at adaptation to, and justification of, a capitalist régime which is in the sharpest contradiction to Christianity. The words of St. Paul, "There is no power but of God" (Rom. xiii. 1), had a fateful influence, although they had no religious, but only temporary, historical significance. The Apostle's words became a source of opportunism. Based on the Christianity of St. Paul, two lines developed: either the ascetic way and flight from the world, which justified an ascetic-metaphysical view-point, or else the way of adaptation to the forces ruling in the world.

Christianity has repeatedly defined its attitude toward forms of social organization made by others, but has never revealed the truth of society organized from the depths of Christianity, itself. The Christian truth about society has not yet been revealed—the times and seasons for that have not yet come. Hence, for the time being, we have to affirm the dualism of "God" and "Caesar", a natural-social dualism, and that of society and the state. This is a source of freedom, but this is not final: this is dualism *en route*, temporary. The final point of orientation must be the Kingdom of God, in which all dualism is overcome.

We must also make clear the difference between society and *a* society, a community. To organize a society, in which there is always a large element of necessity, does not mean the creation of communality. In the next chapter we shall speak of the profound difference between the idea of religious "together-ness" (*sobornost*) and the socialist idea of collectivism. The final goals of man's life are not social, but spiritual. On the other hand, the distinction between an individually-moral and a socially-moral act, is quite false. One cannot be a man of good morals and a good Christian in his individual, personal life, and be a cruel exploiter and a-moral in social life in his quality as a representative of public authority, proprietor of an enterprise, head of a family, etc. Equally false and anti-human is the distinction between a man and his hierarchic rank, the substitution of hierarchical office for man himself. The chief reason for the crisis of Christianity and of society, and for the decline of faith, lies in the concept of Christianity as exclusively a religion of personal salvation. On the basis of such a concept it is impossible to solve the problems of relationship between man and society. Only a new concept of Christianity, only comprehending it as a religion, not alone of personal, but also of social and cosmic transfiguration, that is by an increased sense of messianism and prophecy in Christianity, can bring a solution to the tormenting problems of relationship between man and society.

\*
\* \*

The problems of relationship between man and society have become more acute because of the role played by socialism in the life of the world. The word "socialism" itself derives from the word "society". In the days when socialism was still a poetic dream, and had not yet become the prose of life and authority, it thought it would be organized humanity. Even Marx thought that socialism was to set up a new society for the sake of man. The fateful dialectic of everything which is set up in the world, in the realm of Caesar, had not yet become evident. But regardless of the practical truth in socialism, at least its critical truth as regards capitalism, the metaphysic of socialism is false. This metaphysic is based on the primacy of society over human personality, even on the supposition that man can only gain by this primacy. Socialism may go two ways: it can create either a new society or a new slavery. The depth and truth of socialism is that human personality in general, and specially that of the worker, must change from object to subject. The basic contrast remains, between personality and the material. We cannot admit that man should be considered as a thing, as object. Man is subject and personality, and that social system is justified which recognizes this. Of the distinction between socialism and communism we shall speak later, in the chapter on collectivism and Marxism.

It has been said that the difference between socialism and communism is that of the motto of socialism is "from each according to his capacity, to each according to his labour", while the motto of communism is "from each according to his capacity, to each according to his need". This is a secondary, not a principal distinction: it merely indicates different degrees of the acquisition of wealth by society. Another distinction is far more fundamental, namely that socialism does not demand a totalitarian view-point, as does communism, neither does it strive toward the collectivization of man's whole personal life, nor does it consider all means as permissible. But social-ism, too, in most cases based on a false metaphysic, recognizes the objective world as a prime reality, and the subjective world as secondary. This is one of the trans-formations of the realm of Caesar. Materialism, i.e. the absolutization of things and objects, is an inheritance from the bourgeois world-outlook. Capitalism is practical atheism. There is much truth in what Ragatz says on this doctrine. But he is in error when he thinks that infinity has been revealed to the proletariat because it is free of possessions. Socialism is always threatened with being made bourgeois, as Herzen so sharply pointed out. And in the spiritual sense of the word, communism also may be bourgeois. The most profound difference is not with capitalism, as an economical category, but "bourgeois-ness", as a spiritual and moral category. The revolu-tionary element in social struggle for a new society is usually determined, not by its social ideals, not by the spiritual and moral changes in the people who are creating this new society, but rather by the means they use and the degree of violence employed. Gandhi was of course more revolutionary than the communists, in the spiritual sense of the word, and just because of this spiritual revolution he was killed.

In this whole connection one's attitude toward time is

of great importance. Can one consider the present as a means to the future, and the present generation as a means to generations yet to be? It is often thought that revolutionary socialism in the present generation of living men is simply a means to a future end. Hence it is considered permissible to kill off great numbers of people, cause limitless suffering, in order to realize human welfare and happiness in the future. Thus men have always set up the realm of Caesar, and are still doing so: this is the law of Caesar's realm. Differences here are only of degree. Revolution is conceived as anti-personalism.

Socialism's most difficult problem is that of freedom. How can one combine the solution of the problem of bread for everyone, a problem on which human life itself depends, with the problem of freedom, on which human dignity depends? On the basis of materialism, the problem is insoluble, it can be solved only on the basis of religious socialism. The tragedy of the situation lies in the fact that human masses are passing through a process of de-christianization and materialism, for which process Christians themselves are to blame. By itself alone, socialism will never create either the perfect society or social equality. It may be that the sinful forms of the exploitation of man by man will disappear, or that classes in the sense that they have been created by the capitalist system will be no more. But there will be formed a new, privileged ruling class, a new bureaucracy—what we now call the "organizers" (James Burnham).

A dual process is taking place in history: a process of

socialization and one of individualization. Communism tends toward a totalitarian socialism: that is its special characteristic. But communism's economic system does not have to be a totalitarian socialization of human life. This derives from the philosophical world-outlook of communism, from its religious faith. This is its chief difference from socialism. Socialism is less spiritual: it involves a process of individualization. But socialism may be considered as a generic term, and then various forms of socialism are possible. You may have revolutionary or reform-socialism, religious or atheistic, socialism democratic or aristocratic. Here we are speaking not of social changes in Europe, but of principles. There has always been a chiliastic element in socialism; it is found both in utopian socialism and in that of Marx. But just this unrecognized chiliastic and messianic element in socialism gives rise to fanaticism, and with this is connected its militant, anti-religious character. But just this extreme hostility toward religion may itself be a longing for religion. This is what we have in that special variety of socialism known as communism. The word socialism itself is colourless and almost without meaning: it comes from the word "society". The word communism is more significant: it is connected with belonging to something, with the idea "community". But in actual practice communism becomes not so much communal as collectivizing. We shall see that this is its basic distinction. If it were not for the transformation of communism into extreme collectivism, which leaves no place for individualization of any kind, I would have preferred the word "communism", and I would have stood for a religious and aristocratic communism (not in the social, but the classic sense). But in view of what life has done to terminology, I prefer the word "socialism".

It must be recognized that socialism is more restrained in the means it uses, less inclined to attain its ends through violence. And in the past, chiliastic, Christian communism, striving to realize the Kingdom of God on earth, was inclined to violence and blood. In this connection the figure of Thomas Münzer is revealing. Communist utopias such as those of Campanella or Cabet, pictured an ideal system where there was no room for freedom, and where the organization of society was tyrannical. In reality, the problem of socialism—the question of bread and social justice—is elementary and relative. Socialism, if we use the term in the radical sense, can never solve the basic problems of human existence. After the elementary truths of socialism have been realized, there will appear with special clarity, man's most profound problems, and the tragedy of human life will become specially poignant. The purposes of human life are spiritual, not social: the social is relative only to means.

Now the struggle against a bourgeois society and a bourgeois spirit, in which communism and socialism are not sufficiently active, does not mean that we deny the positive values of the bourgeois and humanistic period in history, period which affirmed freedom of thought and of science, abolished torture and cruel punishments, recognized a greater humaneness. In this connection the XIXth century was a great century. The idea of a proletarian culture, which by the way neither Lenin nor Marx affirmed, is thoroughly absurd. A proletarian psychology and culture could mean only man's enslavement. Culture can be only all-human, and inevitably implies an element of the aristocratic. Equally absurd is the idea of the religion of labour. Work has a religious sense, but its end and aim is liberation from the heaviness of labour. This will be one of the achievements of technics, once it is made subject to spirit. But socialism must imply a new, not bourgeois attitude toward life, new and not bourgeois attitudes of man toward man. This is not merely a social task, it is above all spiritual, a spiritual revolution. We must desire the development and the triumph of religious socialism, but this does not mean a religion of socialism. Subjecting socialism to religious elements and purposes is liberation from the false religion of socialism, from the false objectivation of society.

# CHAPTER IV

# MAN AND CAESAR—AUTHORITY

CAESAR IS THE ETERNAL symbol of authority, the state, the kingdom of this world. Two basic views are possible, as regards the mutual relationship between Caesar, authority, the state, the kingdom of this world on the one hand, and spirit, man's spiritual life, the Kingdom of God, on the other. This relationship may be conceived either dualistically or monistically. We have already spoken of the relative truth of dualism in the conditions of this present world. Monism, whether religious or anti-religious, always tends toward tyranny. But rightly understood, the dualism concerning the kingdom of Caesar and the Kingdom of God, of spirit and nature, Spirit and society organized in the state, may provide the bases for freedom. Wrong have been the understanding and the interpretation of the Gospel's "Render unto Caesar that which is Caesar's, and unto God that which is God's" and the words of St. Paul: "There is no power but of God".

There has been a slavish interpretation of these words. "Render unto Caesar . . ." does not mean a religious definition of Caesar and his realm; it does not imply evaluation at all. This is merely distinguishing between two different spheres which cannot be combined one with the other. The expression "There is no power but of God" which has been of really fateful significance has all too often meant servility and opportunism in relation to the authority of the state and the sacralization of forms of authority which were anything but Christian. The Apostle Paul's words have no religious meaning whatever: they are purely historical and relative, called forth by the position of Christians in the Roman Empire. St. Paul was afraid that Christianity might turn into an anarchistic, revolutionary sect. He wanted to place Christianity into universal history. We must recall, further, that some time later, during the reign of Domitian, the state authority was called the beast from the abyss.

The problem is vastly more complex than those who cite St. Paul's words usually think. In the past, Christianity has frequently shown not a little servility to the realm of Caesar. This usually followed a regular formula: Any change, revolution or reform, in the realm of Caesar, at first aroused opposition on the part of the Church, condemnation of the novelty as an apparition of the spirit of Antichrist. But when the new power of Caesar became stabilized and confirmed, the Church suddenly noticed that this authority was also from God, and proceeded to sanction it. Thus it turned out that the Church only sanctioned what others had wrought, other forces outside the Church and Christianity, and had no ideal of her own for society and the state. And things were worse when the Church seemed to have her own ideal, in the

Christian theocracies of history, because these theocracies were Christian only in name, and in reality they denied freedom. Theocracies were one of the temptations through which Christianity had to pass. This was not limited to theocracy in the mediaeval sense of the word, but included "Christian" states, which were always Christian only in a symbolic, not a real sense, and which compromised Christianity. The depth of the problem lies in this, that spirit cannot be dependent upon nature and society, nor be determined by them. Spirit is freedom, but in the objectivation of spirit in the course of history, a series of myths were created which were used to confirm the authority of government. Such myths as that of sovereignty in the religious sphere, the infallibility of the Pope, or that of a council of bishops. In the life of the state and of society there have been myths: the myth of monarchy, the sovereign power of the monarch, the myth of democracy—the sovereign power of the people (*Volonté générale*), the myth of communism—the sovereign power of the proletariat. Although it has not always been openly acknowledged, all these myths in reality are mystic in their nature, and, as a rule, they have contained not a new understanding of the myth of sovereignty, but the denial of the very idea of sovereignty. Sovereignty belongs to no one: it is only one of the illusions of objectivation.

\*
\* \*

It may be said that my view-point is too much under
the influence of the anarchist myth, but this is not the
case. The idea of a utopia, happy and stateless, is quite
foreign to me. Under the conditions of this world, the
function of the state will always remain. But the state is
of functional and subordinate importance, only. What we
must refuse, is the sovereignty of the state. The state has
always tended to reach beyond its normal boundaries,
and to become an autonomous sphere of life. The state
wants to be totalitarian. This applies not only to communism and fascism. In the Christian period of history
we see a return to the heathen concept of the state: a
totalitarian and monist concept. One of the classic arguments of Celsius against the Christians is that they are not
loyal citizens of the state, that they feel they belong to
another kingdom. We have this same conflict to-day, the
eternal conflict between Christ the God-Man, and Caesar
the man-god. The inclination to deify Caesar is always
present, it is revealed in monarchy, but may also appear
in democracy or in communism. Christianity cannot be
reconciled to the sovereignty of any kind of earthly authority—not the sovereignty of a monarch, not that of the
people or of a class. The only principle reconcilable with
Christianity is the assertion of man's inalienable rights.
But the state recognizes these unwillingly. And even the
principle of the rights of man has been deformed: instead
of implying the rights of the spirit against the wilfulness
of Caesar, it was included in Caesar's realm and came to
mean not so much the rights of man as a spiritual being,

as it did the rights of a citizen, that is of a partial being.

The struggle goes on between monism and dualism. Monism is always turning back to the heathen concept of state authority, while dualism is of Christian origin, confirmed by the blood of the martyrs. The relationships between dualism and monism are paradoxical. The theme of social revolution includes extreme elements of both. It is dualistic in its division of the world into two parts, those for and those against the social revolution, and monistic in its affirmation of its own reign. The social revolution also contains, however, an element of the chiliastic and messianic: it is striving for the Kingdom of God on earth, although without any belief in God. And this leads to monism, the refusal to recognize the distinction between the realm of Spirit and that of Caesar. The realm of Caesar is transient: that of the Spirit is everlasting. The duality in the psychology of social revolutionaries merely proves that monism, one-ness, may be conceived only eschatologically. There is a type of secularized eschatology which deifies not eternal life, but merely life in the future. The relation between church and state is one of the forms of relationship between Spirit and Caesar, but in the shape of historical objectivation. In the course of history, the church has easily accepted the realm of Caesar, the realm of objectivation, but another element always persisted. Caesar belongs to the objectivized world: he is subject to necessity. But Spirit belongs to the realm of freedom. The relationships between church and state have been, and always will be, contradictory and they present an insoluble problem. The conflict is not resolved even when an opportunist church adapts itself to the state. Church politics have often been adapted to the realm of Caesar. The Emperor Constantine was an important factor in this process. In its symbolics, the Empire became Christian. But what was more significant, the Church became imperial. The teachers and Fathers of the Church ceased to be the defenders of freedom of conscience, which they once had been. The spirit is limited by Caesar: the two realms coalesce. The Church consecrates Caesar. The ecumenical councils˙ are . assembled by the Byzantine emperor whose position is accepted as one of the orders of the Church. The two types of Christianity appear, eastern and western, tending, the one toward Caesar-papism and the other toward papo-caesarism.˙The authority of Caesar receives consecration at the hands of the Church. It might even be said that a new sacrament is established, the sacrament of imperial authority. This should have produced a revolutionary uprising, but the recognition of the sacred right of the monarch changes to the recognition of the sacred rights of the people, and then to the right of the proletariat. The idea of sovereignty and of sacred rights remains.

*
*  *


From earliest times men have felt the need for a religious sanction of authority, which sometimes took the

form of the sacrament of anointing. It was felt that, otherwise, the people would not submit to the authority. In
ancient times, "man" and "citizen" were synonymous.
Religion was tribal and national. It had a special character in ancient Israel. This was the only serious and
profound form of racism. Race had a religious significance. But the tribal-national, racial character of Hebrew
religion involved the recognition of the Jewish people
as elect, the people of God, and hence it included elements of universality. Messianism is always universal. In
the pre-Christian world there was a tendency toward
making politics and morality synonymous. For our
present theme, the apotheosis of the Roman emperors is
more significant. This went beyond the limits of con-
secrating authority. It is directly related to our modern
dictators, who are more sacred persons than ever were
kings or czars. The reform of Caesar Augustus was an
attempt at religious reform in Rome, and the regime
which Augustus tried to set up was a totalitarian regime.
Augustus was Pontifex-Maximus, and he united in himself two elements, Caesar and spirit. It was decided that
Caesar Augustus was descended from the gods. The cult
of Caesar strengthened the position of Rome. In the
heathen consciousness there was no impassable boundary
between the gods and man. The Emperor Augustus was
not considered as a case of deification of one certain man.
In the man-emperor, his genius, in the antique meaning
of the word, was worshipped. There is a difference
between *divus* and *deus*. The authority of a caesar or

even of a czar is really of heathen derivation and is in principle foreign to Christianity. Celsius defended the empire and the apotheosis of imperial authority against the Christians using arguments which closely resemble those used nowadays to defend the totalitarian state. The apotheosis of Caesar is the source of totalitarianism in its extreme forms. This is the subjection of spirit to Caesar. We must remember that the apotheosis of the caesars, as well as of all tyrants and dictators since, was the work of the people, the poor, rather than of the senate, which was always sceptic and little inclined towards mystic beliefs. We frequently forget that the Greco-Roman world did not know the principle of freedom of conscience which the dualism of spirit and Caesar presupposes. And toward the end of the antique world, freedom had disappeared altogether. But the terrible fact is that the cult of emperors continued in the Christian world. This is specially notable in Byzantium; this made it a not-quite-Christian empire. Bishops in the Middle Ages sometimes repeated what had been said to emperors in the Roman senate: "You are the image of Divinity", but the West attempted to limit the power of Caesar by means of the Church.

The Middle Ages are characterized by the idea of organic unity. *Omnibus multitudo derivatur ab uno.* Every part presupposed the unity of a whole. Humanity is one, and forms a mystic body. But on the other part, the deification of the state was not characteristic of mediaeval thought. Herein the West had the advantage over the East. The state was set up by an act of violence in the sinful world, and only tolerated by God. The biblical idea of the origin of royal authority is very unfavourable to it. Royal authority arose against the will of God, and if we think it through to the end, we must admit that from God proceeds only freedom, and not authority. Mediaeval Christianity's consciousness did not recognize the unconditional submission to the state by its subjects. It was considered permissible not to submit to tyrannical authority. The possibility was even admitted of tyrannicide. At the same time the absolute importance was recognized of natural law, which proceeds from God. The government ought to serve the people. A whole series of mediaeval Christian theologians, philosophers and jurists recognized the innate and inalienable rights of the individual (Gierke). In this point the mediaeval consciousness was superior to that of our day. But that consciousness was contradictory: capital punishment for heretics was accepted. Slavery was considered to be the result of sin, rather than sin itself. The history of Christianity has seen terrible abuse of the idea of original sin: from it the most slavish deductions have been made. Even Melanchthon defended the killing of heretics; Calvin executed Servetus; and Theodore de Bèze stands against the freedom of conscience. The empire came to the East from the West, hence the process of absolutizing authority was more intense in the East than in the West. Dualism was always stronger in Catholicism than in the East, where monism was predominant. But we must note that the contradictory relationships between the realm of Spirit and that of Caesar are deeper than the mediaeval conflict of spiritual and temporal power.

*
*  *

A confusion between the realm of Caesar and the Kingdom of God, or even making them identical, has always existed in practical life, in thought and doctrine. Men have had an irresistible tendency toward monistic and totalitarian systems. The theocracies were like this, and in a particularly extreme form, the Byzantine theocracy. But the democracy of Rousseau and the Jacobins was equally monistic and totalitarian. We meet the same identification of the two realms and the two orders in Hegel, Marx, Auguste Comte, Spann; in communism and in fascism. The so-called liberal democracies, which claimed to be neutral in regard to the realm of Spirit, no longer exist: they have increasingly become dictatorships. The disappearance of the neutrality of the realm of Caesar is an important moment in history. Caesar has increasingly more to say on questions of Spirit, even if it takes the form of a radical denial of spirit: where once the emperors said that they were called not only to rule the state, but to look out for the salvation of the souls of their subjects, the caesars of to-day are also concerned with saving souls, if only from religious superstitions. Caesar always and irresistibly tends toward demanding for himself not only that which is Caesar's, but that which is

God's—Caesar wishes to subject to himself the whole of man. This is the main tragedy of history, the tragedy of freedom and necessity, of man's fate and historic destiny. The state, attempting to serve Caesar, is not interested in man: man exists for the state only as a statistical unit. And when the state begins to be much interested in man, it enslaves him, not only externally, but internally as well, although the realm of Spirit cannot be contained within that of Caesar. Spirit is limitless and moves toward infinity. Caesar, on the contrary, is finite and he tries to place on spirit the seal of his finiteness. Some of Caesar's demands are satisfied by all men living on the earth. We all render unto Caesar what is his, even if it is in the form of revolution in which we participate. The demand for revolution is also a demand of Caesar, but spiritual revolution is something apart, it cannot be involved in political and social revolutions: it belongs to another plane of being. This dualism of Caesar and spirit, while opposed to all monism, should not prevent our participation in the world and the processes going on in it. Spirit breaks irresistibly into the objective world, overcomes its necessity and slavery. This is always a vertical movement, which only later becomes objective and symbolized in the horizontal. Under the conditions of our present world, in our space and time, we cannot conceive of the final victory of spirit over Caesar. There is a continual process of the spirit's becoming lost in the objective world, and spirit has constantly to struggle for a return to its own depths. Hegel, with his historic pantheism, only half understood this. And in this sphere of the alienation and objectivation of spirit, the realm of Caesar establishes itself. In this sphere Caesar changes his shapes, and here authority has functional significance. The final victory of spirit over Caesar is possible only in the eschatological perspective. Until then, men will live under the hypnosis of authority, and this includes the life of the Church, which, itself, may turn out to be one of the forms of Caesar's realm.

\*

\*    \*

The secret of authority, of the subjection of men to those in authority, has not been fully unravelled up to the present time. Why is it that large masses of men, in whose hands is predominant physical force, accept subjection to one man or a small group of men, if they are bearers of authority? Even an ordinary policeman causes a different feeling, when we meet him, than an ordinary mortal in civilian clothes. Just as in ancient times, people to-day are inclined to believe that there is such a thing as anointing to power. Here, of course, remnants of the slavery of earlier times come out, relics which have not been fully eliminated even in democracy. It has frequently been said that the exercise of authority is connected with hypnotism. State authority may rule a people quite rationally, but the origin of authority is quite irrational. The talent of men of authority consists in their capacity to impress others. He rules, who can put popular masses into a hypnotic state. Here propaganda, which is a vulgar form of hypnotism, plays a great role. And if people were not capable of being hypnotized, no one knows how long any authority could maintain itself. A more profound situation existed when authority was based on the religious faith of a people: and the historic forms of this authority collapsed when this faith disintegrated. This must be said of the divine monarchies of the past. Democracy, on the other hand, maintains itself chiefly by the propaganda and rhetoric of the politicians. We witness the objectivation of men's psychic condition, rooted in the depths of not only individual, but a collective subconscious. The sub-conscious may take on forms of consciousness which are surprising for their irrationality. The whole process takes place in the complex interreactions of human groups. That opinion errs, which holds that political life is the most selfish feeling of individuals and social groups. The so-called interest of social groups is very often irrational and opposed to every sound reasoning. A group of great capitalists may wish to cause a war: the force of capitalism automatically moves them in this direction. But the war may bring about the destruction of these capitalists, their capital, and the whole régime. It may be said that the irrational always lurks in selfish interest. Men are moved not so much by reasoned interest as by passion. Those forms of authority developed by history are always objectivized and rationalized sub-conscious states and passions. And this always

means the creation of myths, without which it is impossible to govern human masses. One or another myth of
sovereignty is created.

In modern times, an attempt has been made to ration-
alize the origin of authority, by means of the theory of
social contract. With Hobbes and his pessimistic views of
human nature, this led to the affirmation of monarchy,
while in Rousseau, optimistic in his view of human
nature, it led to the affirmation of democracy. But in
reality neither contract nor rational explanations are
important: all forms of authority are based on sub-
conscious collective feelings and passions, unless they
are based on religious belief. With Bossuet the absolute
authority of the state and the absolute power of the monarch are based on religious sanction, although this was
in contradiction to Catholicism, always more inclined
toward a dualistic system. The false idea of sovereignty
was transferred from the monarch to the people. When
Louis XIV said "I am the state", the revolutionary
people answered: "We are the state". But it is still the
same false principle of sovereignty. It is interesting to note
that the idea of popular sovereignty arose in the monas-
teries: it was affirmed by the Catholic theologians Suarès
and Bellarmin. This is a negative ideology: a higher,
more positive ideology is that there is no such thing as
sovereignty. We have already spoken of the difference
between the ancient and modern concepts of freedom.
But the idea of popular sovereignty is a return to the
ancient conception. This appears in the various forms of

social doctrine. Cabet, who considered himself a Christian communist, in his perfect utopian sphere, denied freedom of the press. Louis Blanc insisted upon a completely authoritarian socialism hostile to freedom. Hegel absolutized the state as the incarnation of spirit, and this influenced the absolutization of society in Marxism. Montalembert was not altogether wrong in stating that democracy is opposed to freedom of conscience. Proudhon is an exception to all the social thinkers: for him the central idea is human worth, which is justice. Proudhon was an enemy of violence, and he defined revolution as the enlightenment of men's minds. Because he did not wish to transfer sovereignty from one subject to another, he was considered an anarchist, but in this he was right. We must clear our minds of the myths of authority, always based on the sub-conscious. There is only one great myth, about one great reality: the myth of man, of his freedom, his creative energy, his likeness to God and his communal relationships to his kinsfolk and to all men.

The origin of authority is doubtless connected with the existence of evil. And this in a double sense. Authority is obliged to struggle against the manifestation of evil: that is its function. But it, itself, produces evil and extends it. And then a new authority becomes necessary, to put a limit to the first. And then, again, the authority which has just put an end to one evil, itself becomes evil. And there is no escape from this vicious circle. Conquest and lordship always involve a dialectical regeneration and transformation into the opposite of that for which the struggle was waged. This is the outcome of every revolution. Revolution fights against an authority which has become evil, and in its struggle for power those come out on top who are most capable of organizing authority, crowding out and often destroying those less capable. Revolution reveals both the heights of human nature and its depths: passionate devotion to an idea, neglect of selfish interest, and cruelty, ingratitude, the destruction of high spiritual values. This is man, in his contradictions.

We must have the courage to admit that in Christianity there has been no revelation about society. This revelation, as I have said before, must come in the epoch of the Holy Spirit. This is why all the efforts, hitherto, to set up a new and better society, have finished so tragically. The problem of society is a problem of relationships, not between "I" and "Thou", but between "I" and "We" and through the relation to "We", the relation to "Thou". But "We" has remained an inhuman anonymity, which was ruthlessly ordered about by both "I" and "Thou". "We" has been an objectivation of human existence. The power of "We" over all human "I"'s did not assume human relationships between them, and this is true for all sorts of régime. The liberation of man was only relative, only in its negative phase, and did not comprehend the whole man. Thus, for instance, liberalism freed human thought and science, freed men from the external authority of the Church, but they did not liberate the working man from the camouflaged power of capital. And the liberation of the workers from the power of capital may lead to the enslavement of thought. Every authority, openly or in disguise, has poison within itself. True liberation will come only with the elimination of the idea of sovereignty, regardless of the subject to which this sovereignty applies. The constant chaos caused by struggles for the self-determination of peoples provokes wars, while humanity in all ages has longed for the elimination of that chaos and dreamed of universal unity. We may conceive of three ideas, a world-empire (the Roman Empire, the Empire of Charlemagne, Napoleon's Empire), a multitude of sovereign nations struggling for equilibrium, and a world federation of free nations surrendering their sovereignty and accepting the authority of a world-organization. We should strive only for this last, but this will mean radical changes, both spiritual and social.

# CHAPTER V

# OF THE HIERARCHY OF VALUES.
## ENDS AND MEANS

MAN IS A BEING which estimates and defines quality. The definition of values and their arrangement in hierarchic order is a transcendental function of consciousness. Even the savage judges values. But in our world the hierarchy of values has been upset, the lower have been put on top, the higher suppressed. This is true not only of Soviet Russia, but perhaps more so of America, yes, of all of Europe. The life of human societies proceeds under the sign of the domination of economics, technics, deceitful politics, blatant nationalism. The accepted hierarchy of values is fixed according to their usefulness, quite regardless of truth. Spiritual culture is suppressed. The question rises not only of values created by man, but of the value of man himself. The real aims of human life have been dimmed. Man has ceased to understand why he is living: he has not time to meditate on the meaning of life. Man's life is filled with means for living, which means have become ends in themselves.

This substitution of means for life itself is a very characteristic process, which explains many things in human life. A clear instance of this is the determinative role of economics, which captured the thought of Marx. But, indisputably, economics belong to the means and not to the ends of life. There is a division, so great as sometimes to eliminate all resemblance, between the purposes of human life and the means by which these purposes are realized. This is one of the products of objectivation, which always causes division, and is subject to necessity. That cause should give rise to effect in the world of phenomena, is in effect an abnormal thing. This leads to the fact that in the baser conditions of this world, force and violence must be exerted for the realization of any ends. It is characteristic that no one ever proposes evil ends: evil is always disguised as good, and detracts from the good. This becomes evident only in the means employed. These means always give evidence of the spirit of the men who use them, the spirit of freedom or slavery, of love or hate. There is always danger in the realization, at all costs, of any given purpose. If, to achieve a truly just social system and final human felicity, you have to torture and kill several millions of people, the chief question is no longer the aim, but of the means employed: the aim withdraws into the dim distance, while the means are the immediate reality. Dostoevsky put it very sharply in his question whether it would be right to achieve paradise on earth at the cost of one tear of one innocent and tortured child. And among the millions who have been martyred for the sake of future blessedness, there are certainly many innocent.

The principle that the end justifies the means, was not invented yesterday. Although it used to be attributed to the Jesuits, it has been used by too many others. The main consideration is this: not that the means are a-moral, cruel, not comparable with the high aim in view, but rather that, when evil means are employed, means which even contradict the ends sought, these ends are never attained: the means take central place, and the ends are either forgotten, or become purely rhetorical. The evil means form men's souls, while the good ends lose their living force. Hence the empire of falsehoods in which man is submerged. In the past the good ends of Christianity have too often been realized by the wrong means. The attempt was made to implant Christianity in Europe by blood and violence. Orthodoxy in Byzantium was connected with bestial cruelty. The pyres of the Inquisition, the massacre of St. Bartholomew, the denial of freedom of conscience and thought, and many other such things, are fresh in our memories. These evil means have led to the degeneration, rather than the strengthening of Christianity. The good ends of the French Revolution, liberty, equality and fraternity, were also achieved by violence and terror which raged throughout the Revolution. And the result was the capitalist system of the XIXth century, in which there was no equality and even less fraternity. The Russian communist revolution also employed terror, and up to now it has created neither brotherhood nor a communal society. Freedom is never achieved by violence, brotherhood through hatred, peace by bloody conflict. Evil means are poisonous. The autumn of revolution never resembles its spring. In practice, the use of evil means against the enemy is always declared permissible, for the enemy is no longer considered human. And the inescapable, vicious circle is formed. Christ's words about loving our enemies offer escape from this vicious circle of hatred. When hatred and revenge are invoked for the sake of liberation, enslavement is the result. The organization of a more just and happy society is not an end in itself, it is only a means toward a worthful human existence. Humanity's aim remains the higher values, but these predicate humanized means. The end is meaningful only if we begin its realization here and now.

*
*   *

There are two kinds of philosophy: Philosophy of value, and philosophy of usefulness or good. Value is quality: the philosophy of quantity is more prevalent. Marxism is a philosophy of goods and not of values. You cannot talk with Marxists about the hierarchy of values, for they do not understand your putting the question: for them only necessity, "good", usefulness, exist. Nietzsche's philosophy, in contrast to that of Marxism, is a philosophy of values. For Nietzsche man is above all a creator of values. But his philosophy of values is contradictory and unjustifiable, on account of its biological tendencies and his vision of the meaning of life in the will to power. Pushkin's verse presents vividly and powerfully the contrast between the creative freedom of the poet and the utilitarian demands of the masses, although for him the "masses" were probably the lesser aristocracy, the bureaucrats, rather than the workers. The masses may change their social make-up. In passionate defence of creative freedom, the poet addresses the mass:

"His (the poet's) song is free as the wind"—"You (the mass) value more a cooking pot: the only kind of food you know"—Pushkin spoke words which caused such indignation in the sixties:

> "But we are born for inspiration
> For music and the sound of prayer."

and again:

> "Thou poet, value not the people overmuch
> Thou art a king, live to thyself alone:
> Where the free spirit leads,
> Pursue thine own untrammelled way."

But the same Pushkin recognized his service to his people and hence foresaw how he would be valued by future generations. We cannot read his lines without emotion:

> "My monument, not made by hands, I've built,
> To which the world will tread a beaten path."

"My fame will spread throughout the whole of Rus . . ."

"And always they will lovingly remember
I roused their tender feelings with my lyre,
Sang songs to freedom in our cruel season,
And mercy for the fallen did inspire. . . ."

Service is not in opposition to creative freedom: it cannot be forced, and loses all its value if it is the result of violence. One of the worst of evils is a utilitarian attitude toward truth. Truth is not the servant of man, and can never be justified by its usefulness: Man is called to serve the truth. The acceptance of economics as the determinant factor in human life had fateful significance in the matter of the hierarchy of values. Economic materialism considers economics as the basic reality, over against which it sets the illusion of consciousness. But this is evidently based on confusion: economics is only a necessary condition and a means for human living; it is not the end, not life's highest value nor its determining cause. Without food, shelter and clothing, I cannot philosophize, but these conditions in no way define philosophy. Materialism's theses that the higher is an epiphenomenon of the lower, and explained by it, is both thoroughly false and quite unconvincing. For the materialist, everything noble in human life, whatever determines its value, must be considered an illusion of consciousness to be unmasked. All of this is a degradation of man. The higher aims of life are neither economic nor social, they are spiritual. The greatness of a people, its contribution to human history, is determined not by its power as a state, not by its economic development, but by its spiritual culture. Germany was at her greatest, and represented the height of European culture, not under the Empire of Bismarck, but when it consisted of a number of small states. The great culture of Greece came out of a small state. The mighty creative movement of the Renaissance in Italy came at a time when that country was breaking up. The high creativeness of Russian culture of the XIXth century, it is true, was under the Great Empire, but it was all directed against the Empire. Creativeness of spiritual culture is not at all in proportion to the political and economic power of leading states.

\*
\* \*

Revolution, in the life of peoples, is a fatum: its course is not determined by freedom, it partakes of the irrevocable. This is usually not well understood by those who live in a time of revolution. Being a mass movement, revolution cannot but debase quality: it always upsets the established scale of values. Revolution throws away many values because of their wrong use in the past. You cannot put down a revolution: you must out-live it, carefully defending spirit, against which revolution always raises its hand. But just as revolution denies the creation of spiritual values, so has organized religion of the past, hardened into its own forms. It has often been said that the creation of values is not at all necessary for the soul's salvation into eternal life, and we must admit that this is true. But the creation of values is needed, not for salvation, but for the fullness of the Kingdom of God in heaven and on the earth. Only a legalistic conception sees in Christianity a religion of salvation, alone. This idea is exoteric: in its depths Christianity is a religion of the realization of the Kingdom of God, for individual, social and cosmic transfiguration. There is a great similarity in the attitudes of social revolutions toward creative values. For the realization of social justice, for the abolition of man's exploitation of man, for the creation of a classless society, neither free creativeness, nor philosophy, nor aesthetic values are needed or are necessary: religious and mystical attitudes are harmful, and the aristocratic concept of spiritual culture is in contradiction to the social revolution. All this distracts from the social struggle, interferes with the realization of the one thing most important. We have often heard this, not only in our day, but fifty and seventy-five years ago. On the surface this may seem true, but inwardly, in reality it is absolutely false, and merely reveals the weakness and disruption of man.

In the deeper sense of the word, revolution, if it is not merely a change of coats, as too often is the case, is a complete, integral change of man and of human society. Social justice cannot be realized without truth and beauty. And if, after a social revolution, life is ugly and stands at a very low level of the knowledge of truth, this is proof of its inner corruption. Ugliness is also falsehood. Beauty, as a higher value, is needed for the social reorganization of society, otherwise the human type is distorted; style and form, image and harmony are wanting. A utilitarian view-point considers that all means are justifiable. This is one of the most evil errors in relation to life. There is nothing more evil than the determination to create good, no matter what the cost. Usually, instead of the radiation of good energy which transfigures man and human society, this means, rather, the radiation of evil energy for realizing good ends. But transfiguring truth must be seen, not so much in man's having set himself a noble aim, which he attains by means which are quite unlike that aim, as in his radiation of good energy. Human life is far more replete with means than with ends, which often tend to become more and more abstract. Under the view-point of qualitative values, ends are achieved by means which themselves are considered these values. It is a horrible fact in human life, that good is realized by means of evil, truth by means of falsehood, beauty by means of ugliness, freedom by means of violence. For the attainment of good ends, the most horrible crimes have been committed. There are profound causes for this. Similar utilitarian deformations have occurred in Christianity. To attain the aims of Christianity, violence and blood have been employed, and Christianity has not been any better attained than the aims of revolution using the same methods. This is connected with the problem of time, with the view of the present, not as an end in itself, but as a means to the future, such a future as never will arrive. Force and utility are valued higher than spirit and truth. It has been amply proved that you cannot realize the brotherhood of men without the expression of brotherhood in the means employed. Force and compulsion are permissible only for limiting evil, for the defence of the weak, and this only in struggle against evil exploitations, against aggressive wars of invasion.

*
*  *

The creation of spiritual culture and values, religious, intellectual, moral or aesthetic, is something aristocratic and presupposes a spiritual aristocracy. This spiritual aristocracy can exist, even in a classless society. The disappearance of such an aristocracy would mean the disappearance of quality. Quality is aristocratic. This does not mean that spiritual culture exists only for the few. The work of great creative geniuses as for example Pushkin and Tolstoy is significant of our whole people. Here, however, we must be on our guard against a confusion of ideas which we frequently encounter, nowadays. Creativeness which is significant for a whole people, does not mean collective creation or creation on command. It has nothing to do with collectivism. The creative genius is always individual, subject to nothing and to no one, and in his individual creativeness he expresses the spirit of the people: he even better expresses the spirit of the people, than the people themselves in their collective life. And every creator must be free: he cannot stand compulsion. In freedom he renders his service. When the creative artist is filling a social order, freedom denied, his product can only be futile and uninspiring. Such activity belongs in the realm of the police, and not in that of creativity. Using a rather unpleasant modern expression, we might say that Virgil filled a social order from Caesar Augustus, but he filled it in inner liberty, moved by creative impulse. Only for this reason could he produce a work of genius. The Russian literature of the XIXth century was always a literature of service and of instruction. It makes us smile to see that modern French literature considers "engagement" as something new. In his articles, Sartre often says things, said sixty years ago by Russian critics like Chernishevsky, Dobroliubov, Pisarev, only he expresses them in a more refined form. And in the end we come back to the classic Marxist attitude toward culture and literature. This is the way men attempt to save themselves from a refined decadence. The cultural elite of our time is passing through a severe crisis, and is in danger of being submerged in the mass social movement. This I have said before. Isolation, pride, scorn of others, will lead to ruin. Only our consciousness of being of service can save us. The genius expresses the faith of his people, and at his highest, that of humanity and the world. But there is an opposite danger, that of adaptation and loss of freedom. The creative artist must first of all and above all keep his creative freedom. Only by this freedom will it be possible for him to serve and express the fate of his people. An isolated individualism is just as wrong as a mechanical productive collectivism.

We should omit the word "collectivism" entirely: as we shall see later, it is only a caricature of "community". Community is always free: collectivism always forced. We cannot permit the quality of creativeness to be debased, for the sake of quantity. The task of the creators of culture should be not humiliating adaptation to the social mass-movement, but its ennobling by bringing into it the aristocratic element of quality. A people expresses its calling in the world through its great creative geniuses, not in faceless collectivism. The world's great cultural achievements, such as the Greek tragedy or the Renaissance, the German culture of the XIXth century or the Russian literature of the same epoch, were not produced by isolated individuals for their own pleasure: they were expressions of a free, creative spirit. Serving one's people is at the same time the creative upbuilding of that people. The creation of spiritual culture always means respecting a hierarchy of values, the only hierarchy which can ever be justified. This brings us to the problem of the conflict of the value of justice and the value of freedom, the basic problem of our modern age.

Nowadays there is a great tendency to set social justice over against freedom, and demand a choice between them. These basic values in human society are distributed geographically: the Soviet Union stands for social

justice, America for freedom. Hence a conflict is held to
be inevitable. In all this, freedom seems to be considered
almost synonymous with capitalism. Against such a statement of the problem we must protest with all the force at
our command. Here I am not going to consider the
political problems of the moment, but the eternal question of justice and freedom: the essentials of freedom will
be discussed in the next chapter. But can we consider
freedom as always opposed to justice? Freedom is far
more elementary than justice. First of all, justice *jus* is
not at all a Christian idea, it is a legalistic idea, in
which there is no grace. Christianity revealed not the idea
of justice, but the idea of truth. The wonderful Russian
word *pravda* has no exact equivalent in other languages.
The realization of justice at whatever cost, by means
of force, may be most detrimental to freedom, just as
the insistence upon formal freedom may call forth the
greatest injustice. This is a revelation of the contradictions of human life. We may have the same type of conflict between freedom and love, between love and justice
and so forth. The tragedy in human life is basically not in
the conflict between good and evil but in the conflict
among positive values. A man may sacrifice love for the
sake of freedom, freedom for the sake of social justice, his
scientific calling for the sake of pity, etc. But all this does
not mean that, to organize human society we must refuse
either freedom or justice. We must strive toward a free
and a just society. Without freedom there can be no
justice: that would be justice in the abstract, unrelated to

real people. Justice demands freedom for all men. I may
limit my own freedom out of consideration for others, but
unless I do this freely, it has no value. Forced sacrifice is
valueless. And my refusal of freedom, in the face of the
conflicts of life, can be only an act of freedom. But there
are freedoms which man has no right to refuse, if he
wishes to maintain his own dignity—such are freedom
or conscience, freedom of the spirit. Alienation of conscience cannot be permitted for the sake of anything
else: it has supreme rights. And no social justice, in any
form whatever, can demand denial of the freedom of
conscience.

The problem is further complicated by the fact that
those who deny freedom of conscience, have in view not
only a just society, where man will no longer be exploited
by man, but a fraternal, communal society. Here we face
a great distinction in principle. The law may compel men
to be just, but it cannot compel them to be brothers. Pity,
mercy, love—these are works of grace in freedom, and
not works of a compelling law. The law which compels
justice may be considered as in opposition to freedom,
but not justice itself, and brotherhood still less. Even the
law which compels justice may be protecting freedom
from the wilfulness of man. For example, insistence upon
social justice for the working classes may mean their
liberation from oppression. In the XIXth century men
were fond of talking about the liberation of labour.
Socialism was related to human freedom. If in the XXth
century men prefer to speak of planned economy, of

increased authority of the state over the individual, this is chiefly because we live in an epoch which has been created by two world-wars, and is preparing for a third. We live at a time when revolution is only war in another form. This determines all values. We live in a world so chaotic that freedom seems like a luxury we may not permit ourselves. The problem of justice and freedom is not viewed in its pure form: we see it through a clouded atmosphere. As a matter of fact, in our world of to-day there is neither freedom nor justice. The struggle for the most elementary goods, for the very possibility of living, crowds out the question of values. In the upper spheres of civilization a process of elementarization is going on, which only appears to be complex.

We may conceive three ways out of the crisis which our world is approaching: First the way of fate: the continued dissolution of the cosmos, that of nature or of society, the continued degeneration of the capitalist régime, the triumph of the atom bomb, a chaotic world such as Henry Miller describes, not an incipient but a final chaos, a war of all against all. This would mean the extinction of the world, and we cannot admit that. Second, a forced mechanical order of the collective, an organization which would leave no place for freedom, despotism in command of the world. This also, it is difficult to accept. Third, the overcoming of chaos from within, the triumph of spirit over technics, the spiritual re-establishment of the hierarchy of values, joined with the realization of social justice. Up to now we have a combination of the first and second ways out. The world seems to be entering a period of compulsorily-organized chaos, which shows no sign of real, inner triumph. The third way out, the only one desirable, leads toward human freedom; it cannot be the result of fatal necessity. In the first and second ways, or in the mixture of the two, man seems to be active, but inwardly he is passive. And here there can be no thought of any hierarchy of values. Spiritual values simply do not exist. This means consigning spiritual values to the abyss. One may be equally pessimist in the first, and optimist in the second case. It is quite absurd to demand proof for the existence of spiritual values and their superiority over so-called "vital" values. Spiritual values, first of all, are affirmed by an act of my freedom: the most necessary is not the most valuable. The higher spiritual values disappear, if they are not affirmed in liberty. Man is free to recognize as real only a small, superficial world; he is free to deny his own freedom. The problem of reality is very complex: it appears simple only to the non-philosophical mind. Life takes on depth and meaning only if it is comprehended in the spirit of symbolic realism. The visible world is a symbol of the world invisible. The unseen world is not a reality forced upon us or compelling us; it derives from freedom of the spirit. And what the free spirit creates, is the most real.

# CHAPTER VI

# THE CONTRADICTIONS OF FREEDOM

THE PHILOSOPHY OF freedom begins with a free act before which there is not, nor can there be, existence, being. If we were to begin with being as the basis, and recognize this primacy of being over freedom, then everything, including freedom, is determined by being. But a determined freedom is not freedom at all. Another type of philosophy, however, is possible, which asserts the primacy of freedom, of the creative act, over being. And only this second type is favourable to freedom. But rational definition of freedom is impossible. Bergson also recognized this. Of the two types of metaphysics, the intellectual and the voluntary, the former is always unfavourable, and the latter favourable, to freedom. But voluntary metaphysics, taken by itself, is not yet a philosophy of freedom. What we must decisively affirm is this, that freedom is spirit, and not being. What has been known as essence or substance is a product of the original existential act. Greek intellectual thinking was unfavourable to freedom. Good was determined by reason. The primacy and reign of reason do not recognize freedom.

It is impossible, here, to analyse the complex relationships between freedom, accident, fate, providence and grace, but we must consider one of them: the relationship between freedom and grace. About this theme the most passionate disputes have raged for centuries in the Christian West. But to me it seems erroneous to contrast one with the other. This contrast means the objectivation of grace, and understanding it as the divine necessity acting from without. But what is called grace acts within human freedom, as its interior illumination. We must not confuse the logical necessity in knowing, with necessity in the life of the world; but even in knowing, itself, there is not an exclusive, logical necessity, which occupies only a portion of knowledge. We must recognize the existence of irrational knowing, and that it plays a big role. Only thus is it possible to know the irrational. So-called rationalism includes quite irrational elements. This must be specially said of materialism. Men have attempted to define freedom through a voluntary understanding of it, as an act of causality (e.g. Maine de Biran, Lopatin), but this did not go to the bottom of the problem. To do this we must recognize the existence of an original, uncreated freedom, outside psychological causality. The so-called traditional teaching concerning freedom of the will, has always been something utilitarian and pedagogical. This doctrine defines man's responsibility in both this life, and the life beyond. We must recognize an indifferent freedom, which is only a mechanization of freedom, as quite unsubstantial. The real problem of freedom must be placed beyond all idea of reward and punishment, of salvation or perdition, beyond sin and redemption, beyond the disputes of St. Augustine with Pelagius or of Luther with Erasmus, beyond all discussions of predestination, which must be denied (both as a word and a concept) at the very beginning of our statement of the problem. All this lies still within the limits of the legalistic concept of Christianity, in the sphere of ideas of consecration and justification, instead of the idea of transfiguration. The true problem of freedom is that of creativity. In line with the purpose of this book, I shall be concerned not with the metaphysical idea of freedom as such, but chiefly with its results in social life.

Freedom is often conceived as something static, whereas it must be thought of as dynamic. There is such a thing as the fate of freedom in the world, the existential dialectic of freedom in the world. Freedom may change over into its opposite. Slavery may be born out of falsely directed freedom. The most general definition of freedom, including all partial definitions, is to say that freedom is a definition of man, not from without, but from within, from the spirit. The spiritual element in man is through freedom, and the denial of the spiritual, carried to its logical conclusion, inevitably leads to a denial of freedom. Freedom is rooted in the realm of the Spirit, and not in the realm of Caesar. Caesar does not wish to give freedom to anyone. It can be acquired only through the limitation of Caesar's realm. The objectivized world, which is Caesar's realm, is a world which enslaves. Another distinction often made is that between inner and external freedom. It is said that a man may be inwardly free, even if in chains, or if he is burned at the stake. This is true. But the question of inner freedom is more complex than is usually thought, particularly when there is no interest in man's inner life. Man may be a slave, not only to the outer world, but to himself, to his lower nature. The liberation of slaves, in external society, still does not mean their liberation from inner slavery. Man may become inwardly a slave. This is why revolutions usually do not lead to setting up new, free societies, and always bear within themselves a return to the old society. There is usually less freedom than anything else in revolutions.

Defining freedom as choice, is still a formal definition. This is only one of the elements of freedom. True freedom is not revealed in the moment when a man must choose, but when he has already made his choice. Here we come to a new definition of true freedom. Freedom is the inner, creative energy of man. By freedom, men may create quite new life, new life for society and the world. But it would be erroneous in this connection to understand freedom as inner causality. Freedom lies outside causal relationships. Causal relations exist in the objective world of phenomena. Freedom breaks into this world. Freedom comes from another world: it contradicts and overthrows the law of this world. It is equally wrong to think of freedom only as a means to the realization of collective social order, and as exclusively dependent upon social order. We shall see that the contradictions of freedom in social life depend on whether we have a formal and a real understanding of freedom. A freedom which

becomes too easy and ceases to demand heroic struggle
is deformed and loses its value. A deformed freedom is
expressed only in the negative consciousness. "I am not
being forced." The final expression of such degraded
freedom is "leave me in peace". Freedom is not at all
easy: freedom is difficult and hard. Freedom is not right,
but obligation. The liberals usually think of freedom as
right, and not as responsibility, and for them freedom
is ease, and the absence of pressure. Hence freedom
becomes a privilege of the ruling classes. In a more profound sense, freedom is man's coming of age, his recognition of his duty, before God, to be a free being and
not a slave.

In contrast to this old, liberal concept of freedom,
stands the heroic concept: freedom presupposes resist-
ance: it is the revelation of power. In order not to remain
a mere formality, the declaration of the rights of man and
the citizen should also be a declaration of their responsi-
bilities. And the accent must be on man as a spiritual
being, which is usually not the case in political revolutions. We know too well, that in a democracy there may
be no true freedom. In the Jacobin democracy, inspired
by Rousseau, there may be confirmed the principles of a
totalitarian state, or of an autocratic national sovereignty.
In capitalist democracies, money and a purchased press
may govern society and deprive it of true freedom, and
this in the face of the fact that the declaration of the
rights of man and the citizen came of religious sources,
was born of the Reformation's assertion of freedom of

conscience. But men have fallen away from this religious base. Hence spirits not truly, inwardly liberated, have created new forms of slave society. False propaganda is continuously violating the masses. Subject to this propaganda, the mass has no inner freedom. The hatred and anger aroused by demagogic propaganda make men slaves, inwardly. And states and parties use these slavish feelings for their own purposes. Under such conditions there can be no suggestion of real democracy. Society will be like the men who compose it.

The basic distinction must be made between freedom as choice, and freedom as a creative act. But there is a still more important, basic question which comes up when freedom is mentioned, and on its solution depends the fate of freedom in our world. And we encounter, here, contradictions which are hard to remove. I mean the problem of the relationship between freedom and truth. Is freedom possible without knowledge of the truth, and is knowledge of the truth possible without freedom? The Gospel says "Ye shall know the truth and the truth shall make you free". This assumes that truth, the real truth, liberates. These New Testament words have been rephrased in the modern world and are repeated by modern totalitarianism, which hates freedom. Thus the Marxist-communists say: "Know the Marxist-communist truth, and it will make you free. Outside this truth there is no freedom: everything is false; there is only a formal freedom affirmed in capitalist societies." Recalling Marxism's connection with Hegelianism, we may say that this knowledge of the truth gives freedom in the form of the knowledge of necessity: freedom is knowledge of necessity. This is just the opposite of Christian freedom. For Christianity, truth is both the Way and the Life. It not only gives freedom, but is revealed in freedom. Freedom is essential for truth. Christianity alone has truly affirmed freedom of the spirit. The truth about freedom was sealed with the blood of the martyrs. Christianity is a religion of the crucified truth. But truth crucified does not force the action of men: its face is toward freedom. And it was treason to Christianity when men tried to make truth compulsory.

Until the end of time, there will always be two kingdoms—Christianity's conflict with the Empire was a struggle of the spirit against Caesar, a struggle which was impossible in pre-Christian, pagan consciousness. Religiously, the pre-Christian man belonged to his nation. And there could be no spheres of life free from society and the state, no freedom of the spirit. This is monism, which cannot truly know what freedom is. Totalitarianism is not something wholly new in our times. Christian theocracy and imperialism were also totalitarian, and monistically denied freedom of the spirit. Napoleon's imperialist régime was a totalitarianism not carried through to its logical end. But in the Christian era, totalitarianism always means a reversion to pagan monism. Hegel's absolute state, as an incarnation of spirit, was also a throwback to paganism. The same must be said of the totalitarian system of Auguste Comte, which might be described as Catholicism without God. Men made God the enemy of freedom, and thought they preserved freedom in liberating men from the idea of God. And historic Christianity has been guilty of this terrible falsehood. The spirit has also been called the enemy of freedom: even materialism has been considered as favouring freedom. A greater aberration it would be hard to imagine. Freedom presupposes the existence of a spiritual element, not determined either by nature or society. Freedom is the spiritual element in man. If man is a being completely determined by nature and society, there can be no freedom. Materialism is the complete denial of freedom, and a social order based on materialism cannot know freedom. We see this in practice. Freedom is first of all, freedom of personality. If you deny the value of personality or doubt its reality, there can be no talk of freedom. Personality is the limit of the power of nature, or of the state, or of society. But personality exists only if man is a free creative spirit over whom Caesar is not all-powerful.

The problem of freedom in its social applications is complicated by the fact that the average man of the masses does not very greatly value freedom. And a mass-revolutionary movement does not strive for freedom, at all. In order that man should struggle for freedom, freedom must already be in him, that is that inwardly he is not a slave. Demagogy, always used to move the masses, deprives people of their freedom: it is psychological compulsion. It is not easy to govern the masses which have

actively entered history. In reality, freedom is aristocratic, not democratic. With sorrow we must recognize
the fact that freedom is dear only to those men who think
creatively. It is not very necessary to those who do not
value thinking. In the so-called democracies, based on
the principle of popular sovereignty, a considerable proportion of the people are those who have not yet become
conscious of themselves as free beings, bearing within
themselves the dignity of freedom. Education to freedom is
something still ahead of us, and this will not be achieved
in a hurry. The old principle of an authority which
limited, or even completely denied freedom has been
shattered beyond repair. Later, however, new authorities
have been set up, sanction for which is sought in the
masses themselves; but these authorities are shaky and
even more difficult and destructive to freedom, than the
earlier ones. We must admit that freedom is more aristocratic, than democratic. At the same time freedom makes
democracy possible. It is a negative value of democracies
that they do not so much limit authority, as transfer it to
a new subject. There was once a bit of truth in liberalism,
but that truth was debased and distorted. Economic
liberalism, as realized in society, became a capitalist
system of *laisser faire, laisser passer*. Least of all favourable
to freedom is the Jacobin concept of democracy.

The contradiction of freedom in social life is also
expressed in the fact that in striving to maintain a given
system, e.g. capitalism, men begin to think of stability
and lack of change as freedom, and movement and

change as its opposite. The class, which in its youth saw freedom as movement, and demanded freedom, in its old age begins to see freedom in non-movement, in stability. The bourgeois classes, inclined to decadence, are apt to see in even the most modest social reforms a violation of freedom. And as a matter of fact, every movement and change produces an alteration in the surrounding milieu, which may seem like compulsion. This only proves that the static idea of freedom is not valid. The static idea of freedom triumphs in the *status quo*. This is a principle of Caesar. And hence we have the strange phenomenon: that reactionaries, hostile to every social change, may present themselves as the defenders of freedom. Against this we must assert the dynamic conception of freedom, freedom as creative movement. But there is always the danger that in the name of freedom, men begin to deny it. Dictators and tyrants refuse freedom to others, but love it for themselves, and always insist upon it for their fellow travellers and those who are connected with them. But he truly loves freedom who affirms it for his fellows.

Another measure for freedom is tolerance, a rare thing, if you take it in its deepest sense. It is quite wrong to identify tolerance with indifferent scepticism. Intolerance has usually been thought of as connected with some powerful religious belief, and national or revolution-ary-social intolerance have been viewed as religious belief transferred to another sphere of life. Fanaticism is an extreme form of intolerance. And tolerant men

are often considered neither hot nor cold. This is a superficial judgment. Fanaticism, which is the extreme form of
intolerance, is the loss of inner freedom. The fanatic is
slave to the idea in which he believes. This narrows his
consciousness, crowds out very important human elements. He ceases to have inner command of himself. The
fanatic cannot connect the idea by which he is possessed,
with freedom, even when he is possessed with the idea of
freedom. Intolerance is a milder form of fanaticism, a
shrunken consciousness, it does not understand the multiplicity and individuality in life. Truth demands freedom, both for him who reveals it and for others as well.
Religious tolerance is connected with the fact that the
truth is limitless, and opens boundless perspectives. Turning truth into finality, which is intolerance or fanaticism,
is treason to truth itself. The intolerant and the fanatic
usually are terribly orthodox, no matter what kind,
Catholics, Orthodox or Marxists, and this orthodoxy produces a petrifaction of beliefs, a paralysis of all movement
of life. Disputation means tolerance: this is something the
orthodox do not accept. Tolerance which is not indifference, is movement toward the infinite. And no single
person has the right to consider himself as possessing the
fullness and finality of truth.

In social life there are degrees of freedom. Freedom
should increase in measure as it approaches spirit, and
decrease as it approaches the material. The greatest freedom is that of spiritual life: the minimum is the freedom
of material existence. Why this should be so, is clear:

since spirit is freedom, while the material is necessity. But there are aberrations: freedom of thought is often denied, while great liberty is granted in economic life. Economics is the working of spirit in the material world, upon which depends the very existence of men in this world's conditions. Absolute freedom in economic life, i.e. its complete autonomy, was the case in the *laisser faire, laisser passer* of the capitalist system. This puts great masses of men into a very difficult situation. It becomes a source of exploitation. Hence in the name of freedom itself, economic freedom must be limited. But as we rise from the material to the spiritual side of life, freedom ought to increase. And while it may occasionally be possible to have an economic or political dictatorship, dictatorship in the realm of spirit and of the intellectual is neither permissible nor justifiable. In times when the question of "bread" (the symbol of economics) for human society is acute, an economic dictatorship may be accepted as necessary. It is claimed that dictatorship in the intellectual sphere is justifiable, since without it, that is, without a world view enforced by the state, the economic dictatorship would be impossible. This is a totalitarian system, which in practice always means that the police control the whole of human life.

The question of right relationships between the two great symbols in the life of society, the symbol "bread" and the symbol "freedom", is difficult and dramatic. When the masses begin to move in a struggle for "bread", they always sacrifice "freedom". Spiritual and intellectual freedom is defended only by a thin cultural layer of society. Further is added the fact that the symbol "freedom" has been misused for evil and not-at-all-liberating purposes. Nevertheless freedom remains the supreme spiritual value, greater than the values of ordinary living. For freedom man may, and should, sacrifice his life: but freedom should not be sacrificed for life. Freedom concerns the quality of human living, the dignity of man. Life unworthy of man is not to be treasured. The working masses naturally prize the material side of life, though this puts them in a position of dependence and does not give them satisfaction. They think and their leaders persuade them, that they are struggling for economic good, recognized as the basis for all living, but by this very fact they should be struggling for freedom. The lack of "bread" is really a lack of "freedom". Failure to solve the economic question makes the realization of freedom impossible. As a matter of fact, we now see that the necessity of social reorganization is accompanied by the reduction of freedom, not merely economic and political, but intellectual and spiritual as well. This concentration on the material side of life, which is the furthest removed from freedom, leads to a situation where men begin to consider the material not as a means, but as an end in itself. Creative spiritual life is either denied altogether, or it is made subject to the material which lays down its directives. The struggle for freedom of the spirit may become heroic. We must keep our faith that after a period of absorption in the material side of life, and the triumph of materialism, a new period will come, cleansed of lower motives and moving toward things of the spirit. In the past, the spiritual was too closely allied to material life which was held to be sanctified by organic life, as though created by God and unchangeable. Nowadays the spirit is breaking away from this bond to the organic life of the flesh. Freedom is based not on nature (natural law), but— on spirit. Ours is a trying and difficult period, one in which the joy of living seems to be diminished.

Freedom is the chief source of the tragic in life. Life in divine necessity would be free of tragedy. But the tragic of freedom must be accepted by man. He has no right to make things easy for himself. And there is no easy solution to the problem of freedom. The two great principles of life, love and freedom, may come into conflict. Freedom may be limited by love, or love by freedom. And this does not always occur harmoniously. In social life, however, we have a conflict of less clear principles: Freedom is limited, not by love, but by economics, which takes upon itself full power. This is sometimes known as the demand for justice, but it cannot always be rightly called that. However, the attainment of monism is conceivable only in terms of eschatology.

# CHAPTER VII

# COMMUNITY–COLLECTIVITY– *SOBORNOST*

THE WORD "COLLECTIVISM" is often used without stopping to think just what it means. The word is usually understood to mean the opposite of individualism. People usually confuse collectivism with community, and do not like it when the difference is called to their attention. Many say proudly that they have entered an epoch of collectivism. Now sometimes a word or a terminology arises by accident. It appears that the word "collectivism" was first used at the socialist congress at Basel in 1869, in contrast to the state socialism of Marxism. Later the word changed its meaning and Marxism itself began to be called collectivism until now Marxism and collectivism are almost synonymous. But it is very important that we fix the difference between "community" and collectivism. Although communism is an extreme form of collectivism, the word "communism" is a better word for it. Although I would wish to eliminate the word "collectivism" for common usage, this is rendered difficult by the fact that the word is used to indicate such entities as army, nation, class, etc., entities which are super-personal. These are collective realities often thought of quite uncritically, in a spirit of realism of concepts. This is always only a process of objectivation and socialization, which mistakes secondary and derivative, for primary, realities. The so-called "collective" realities must of course be recognized as realities, but of quite another order than such realities as the human personality, or even the reality of an animal. "Collective" realities have some existential significance in human life, but not at all that which those would give it, who try to make human personality subject to the collective. We may use collective as an adjective, but not as a noun. Collectivism is *"das Man"*. Such things as collective realities exist, but not "collectives" as realities. A collective is not a reality, but a certain tendency of people or groups, a condition in which they happen to be. Collectivism is a false condition of consciousness which sets up a false reality.

Consciousness sets up many such false realities. The collective does not possess the reality of a nation, for instance, or a class. We often speak of a collective national consciousness, or a collective Church- or class-consciousness, as though a collective could have consciousness. Actually, this is only a metaphysical expression. The so-called collective realities do not have subjective consciousness. There cannot be a Church- or a national-consciousness, a class-consciousness, but there may be such consciousness in the minds of the people who are grouped in these various forms of reality. And this consciousness of these people is then objectivized into a quasi-reality. The Church is without question a reality, a reality of the spirit, a mystic and social-historical reality. But this reality does not predicate some sort of collective above and beyond the personalities who belong to the Church, and possess their own consciousness. The Church has a very great existential meaning in the fate of men, but social objectivation of this reality which is the Church cannot pretend to be a primary reality: it is derivative. The main characteristic of so-called collective realities is that they do not have an existential centre, they can neither suffer nor rejoice. But the capacity for suffering is the mark of truly primary reality. The Church cannot suffer, nor can the nation, or the working-class, it is only the people who form these super-personal entities who can suffer. Within the limits of our fallen world it will always be impossible to reconcile the contrast between the social and the personal. From this fact is derived the despotic power of the "collective" over the personal and individual. We should always remember that we move in a world which is half-illusory, created by wrongly directed consciousness. The error in collectivism inheres in the fact that it would transfer the moral and existential centre, the conscience of man and his capacity to judge and to estimate, out of the depth of human personality over to some quasi-reality which is above and beyond man.

In collectivism man ceases to be the supreme value. This process of the exteriorization of human consciousness has occurred in various forms, throughout history. It is surprising that we hear of the originality of the new collective man, the new collective consciousness, as contrasted with everything personal: this has been

almost the whole of human history. The collective, the
group consciousness has prevailed since earliest times.
Men thought and judged according to their appurten-
ance to the "collective" of tribe, nation, state, family, or
confession. And the consciousness of a man belonging to
the aristocracy or some guard-regiment was no less "collective" than that of the Soviet citizen who thinks of himself as belonging to his communist Fatherland. And
individual thinking and individual judgment have always
been so rare as almost to be exceptions. The awakening
of the personality comes later. And in the so-called
individual, liberal, bourgeois period of history, most
people thought impersonally, made their judgments
according to the bourgeois class, or the form of industry
to which they belonged; thought as did the crowd. What
Heidegger calls "*das* Man" always prevailed—the imper-
sonal domination of "they say". The only originality in
modern collectivism is that it wants to produce a general,
universal collective-human consciousness, thought and
judgment, rather than a varied set of opinions according
to various groupings. To set individualism over against
collectivism is wrong, because the individualism which
they are trying to deny, never existed. If in a bourgeois
capitalist society men's opinions were determined by
their property or their material situation, this would
least of all mean that those opinions were individual or
personal. And a true social liberation would consist in
just this possibility of individual personal consciousness,
thinking and judging. Here we come up against the

definite opposition between collectivism and communality.

Collectivism existed in the historic objectivizations of religion: separately in orthodoxy and in catholicism. And at the other extreme it is revealed in communism and fascism. Collectivism is always evident when in the social life of people the authoritarian principle prevails. Collectivism cannot be otherwise than authoritarian. It cannot admit freedom and communion. Collectivism always means that there is no real community, that for the organization of society it is necessary to set up the fiction of the reality of the collective, from which proceed directives and orders. When the old authority fails, when men no longer believe in the authority of the monarchy or the democracy, then there is set up the authority and sovereignty of the collective, but this always means an absence of inner liberty, a lack of community among men.

What is the principal difference between community and collectivism? Collectivism means the relation of man to man through his relationship to the collective reality or pseudo-reality, to objectivized society, something beyond and above the man himself. Community, on the other hand, means the immediate relation of man to man through God, the inner source of all life. Collectivism refuses to recognize the living relationship of man to man, it desires only man's relationship to society, to the collective, which then determines the relations of man to man. Collectivism does not know the meaning of "neighbour", in the Gospel sense of the word—it is a union of strangers. Collectivism is anti-personal. It does not recognize the value of personality. Community, on the contrary, is personalistic: it represents communion, and the communion of personalities. This is a gigantic difference. Collectivism is a false conception of human relationships. This is the most significant. A "collective" epoch means not only the socialization and collectivization of economic and political life, but of conscience, thought, creativity; there is an exteriorization of conscience, i.e. its removal from the depth of man's being, of man as a spiritual entity, and its transfer to the collective, which possesses the organs of authority. We have a clear and terrifying example of this exteriorization of conscience in the Moscow trials of the old communists. Now to avoid a misunderstanding which might be used for unclean purposes, it must be said at once that placing the organs of judgment and conscience in the heart of man, in his spiritual depth, does not at all mean what is so often known as "individualism". Conscience does not imply man's withdrawal within himself, his isolation from others, but just the opposite, man's victory over egocentrism, his entry into the universal community. But this has no meaning for those who deny that man has spiritual depth, and who consider him only superficially.

Modern collectivism is largely the result of the a-personal, anonymous character of capitalism. Capitalism created the proletarian mass, which unfortunately is more inclined toward collectivism than toward community. Here we approach the Russian Orthodox idea of *sobornost*, so often misunderstood. The idea of sobornost was chiefly expressed by Homiakoff, who connected it indivisibly with freedom and love. Church *sobornost* does not mean authority, not the authority of a Council of Bishops, or even of an ecumenical council: rather it is the communion in love of the church people with the Holy Spirit. While for organizations and societies there are external evidences, no such thing exists for *sobornost*. This is the mysterious life of the Spirit. The "we" in *sobornost* is not a collective: Collectivism is not *sobornost*, but simply being together—(Here Berdyaev makes a play on words: *sobornost—sbornost*—D.A.L.). Collectivism is something mechanical and rational. The objectivation of the passions, interests, hatreds of men or of groups may take the form of a collective. On such a basis, a false mystic of collectivism may be formed, and this may be very dynamic. The chief evil in the formation of a collective consciousness or a collective conscience, is that it is only a metaphorical expression. But the reality hidden behind these words is something quite other. By means of this collective consciousness and conscience, which here takes on a mystical sense, one group of people begins to lord it over other groups. Collectivism is a means for domination, and behind it is hidden the will to power. Real tyranny may be justified by a false mysticism, though the word mysticism is not used, or is even forbidden. Collectivism puts forward its own leaders, and these are not necessarily the best. Leaders in general are rarely of the best. Collectivism is always confirmed by means of violence to the human personality. Community and *sobornost* always recognize freedom and the value of the person.

Community is a spiritual quality of persons, a being-together, a brotherhood of men, and it never means some sort of reality which is above men, or which can order them about. Community leaves judgment and conscience in the depths of man's heart. Consciousness may be at once personal and communal. Community is a quality of personal conscience, which cannot be something closed-up or isolated. Religious community is also called sobornost, something directly opposite to any authoritarian concept of the Church. Collectivism, on the other hand, is alienation, the exteriorization of conscience, attributing this to the fictitious reality of the collective. While *sobornost* means a high quality of consciousness, collectivism means an objectivized consolidation of the subconscious, which has always played a great part in the historic manifestations of collectivism. The objectivation of the Church has often meant an authoritarian collectivism. Religious conscience was transferred to this type of Church collective. Only thus was it possible to deny freedom of religious conscience. *Sobornost*, community, can never mean authority—they always predicate freedom: only collectivism is always authoritarian. And collectivism always means the alienation of consciousness. This alienated consciousness, based on subconscious instincts, has been able, in the past, to set up various historic forms of authoritarism, all the way from theocracy and absolute monarchy, to Jacobin democracy, totalitarian communism and fascism, in open or disguised forms. The state expresses collectivism much more easily than community. It must be firmly kept in mind that personality is not opposed to the social, to society, but only to the thing, the collective. Collectivism is a material, objective way of understanding community. Collectivism is violently opposed to the concept of socialism as something transforming man from object into subject: its tendency is always the opposite, to transform human personality into object. The one justification of socialism is that it wants to set up a form of society in which no single person will be an object, a thing, where each will be a subject and a personality. There are two tendencies in Marxism: the tendency toward objectivation and alienation of man in the collective, and the tendency toward subjectivism, toward the liberation of labour and the labourers from the power of society, a tendency toward humanizing society. Only the second tendency deserves our sympathy: we must struggle against the first. For the first tendency inescapably produces a false, utilitarian religion, the religion of authoritarian collective. There are two tendencies in history: one toward socialization and the other toward individualization. Both are necessary. To-day and to-morrow belong to the socializing tendency: this is in harmony with the necessity of reforming human societies. But the future belongs to the tendency toward individualization. And the spiritual ground for this must be prepared, now.

Man's freedom lies in this, that he belongs to two planes of being: that of the spirit and that of Caesar. Collectivism and the religion which is being built upon it, would confine human life to only one of these planes, that of Caesar. This means monism in the conditions of our present world, the denial of freedom, sheer slavery. Collectivism is something of one plane, only. It moves not toward the transfiguration of this world into the Kingdom of God, but toward the confirmation within the limits of our world of the Kingdom of God, without God, and thus without man, for God and man are inseparably bound together. The confirmation of the human plane alone, inevitably means the denial of man himself. Behind this fact is a fatal dialectic. For concrete examples of all these considerations about collectivism and community, we have only to observe marxism with all its contradictions.

# CHAPTER VIII

# THE CONTRADICTIONS IN MARXISM

WE MAY WELL BE surprised at the role now being played by Marxism. The Marxist doctrine was founded a hundred years ago. It no longer corresponds to either the social realities of to-day or to modern philosophical and scientific thought. Much of it is completely out of date. At the same time, this doctrine continues to be dynamic and even to increase in dynamism. Marxism is particularly out of date in its evaluation of the role of nationality. Two world wars have demonstrated that the Marxist international proletariat does not exist. The workers of all nations have slaughtered each other. Marxist-communists are an unusual, almost mystical phenomenon. They live in a world of their own creation, fictitious, phantasmagoric, mythical, abstract as geometry. They fail completely to see the complexity and variety of the human individual as he really is. At the same time they are very active, and they have aroused the fear of the whole world; some people even believe the Marxists will conquer. Marxist doctrine has been losing its theoretical and apprehensive value, but it has increased in power as a demagogic instrument of propaganda and agitation. The adepts of this doctrine will no more admit a differ-ence of opinion, than will the faithful of religious ortho-doxy. They take any criticism as an attack on them, or a plot against them by the evil forces of capitalist reaction. Like the Manicheans, Marxist-communists divide the world into two parts: and that part of the world which they wish to destroy is, for them, directed by an evil god, against whom all means of action are permitted. There are two worlds, two camps, two faiths, two parties. This is a military division. Variety does not exist: variety is an invention of the crafty foe. So, also, any appeal to any all-human universal code of morals, Christian or humanistic, is an invention of the enemy, in an effort to weaken their adversaries. Hence we have a vicious circle, from which there is no way out.

We must free ourselves from the effects of hatred and fear, and look deeper into Marxist doctrine: many of us know and understand it so imperfectly. The greatest difficulty in comprehending Marxism is that Marxism is interested so exclusively in class, that it does not see the individual: in every thought and estimation of man, the Marxists see only class, with its special class interests. Thought is only an expression of class, and is of no value by itself. Bourgeois-capitalist reason is a different thing from proletarian, communist reason. And there can be no understanding between these two kinds of reason, only war to the death. I think that Marxism is right in its assertion that reason may be modified, that it depends on the type of man's existence, on the integral direction taken by his consciousness. But this must be understood and interpreted in quite another way than that adopted by communism. I have often said that the structure of human consciousness cannot be understood statically, that it changes, broadens or diminishes, and that depending on this change, various worlds are revealed to man. This does not depend on the economic situation of classes, which is of only secondary importance. It is not the discovery of truth that results from a man's class-situation, but rather the deformation of the truth and downright falsehood. Truth is revealed, when man overcomes the limitations of his class-situation, since this class-situation determines not the whole man, but merely some of his aspects. The Marxist concepts of class, the proletariat, the bourgeoisie, and the like, are abstract ideas, which correspond to complex phenomena in the world of social reality. Marxism is characterized by a certain scholastic realism of comprehension, although since they call themselves materialists, Marxists refuse to admit it. The Marxist proletariat is a figment of thought, and only in thought does it exist. In reality there exist only a lot of varied groupings of workmen, and they do not at all possess a unified "proletarian" consciousness. The working class really exists, it is really exploited, and it is carrying on a struggle for its special interests. But the Marxist "proletariat" is the product of a myth-creating process. This is not to say that this myth-created idea cannot be most dynamic in the struggle. On the contrary, myths can be vastly more dynamic than realities. And so it has always been, in history. Abstract ideas, taking the form of myths, are capable of changing the course of history, of radically altering society. All revolutions are based on myths. Conservatism, too, is based on myth, for instance the idea of a consecrated monarchy. Even such a prosaic thing as capitalism is based on the myth of the useful, super-rational natural order and harmony, resulting from the conflict of interests. Marxism contains two different elements, and one of them is primarily dynamic.

The Marxist philosophy is above all a philosophy of history. But the philosophy of history is the most dynamic part of philosophy. The reasons for this are understandable. The philosophy of history always contains within itself a prophetic and messianic element. And the comprehension of the meaning of history is always messianic and prophetic. The philosophy of history taught by Hegel, Marx and Auguste Comte is permeated with this messianic and prophetic fervour. When history is divided into three periods, and the last is considered as the beginning of perfection, this always means secularized messianism. History has not ended yet: we are in the midst of the historic process, and there can be no scientific knowledge about what lies ahead of us. But without such knowledge we cannot learn the meaning of history. Only the light which shines on us from the invisible future can give us understanding of history's meaning, and this light is prophetic and messianic. A philosophy of history based on Greek philosophy was impossible: it is possible only on the ground of Judeo-Christianity, although this has rarely been recognized. Messianism may be unconscious, unadmitted. This is evident in Marxism, which has a strong messianic element. It is not the scientific consciousness of Marxism which gives it a revolutionary dynamic, but its messianic expectation. Economic determinism is powerless to call forth revolutionary enthusiasm and give inspiration for the struggle. The enthusiasm in Marxism comes from the messianic idea of the proletariat, of a liberated humanity. All the qualities of the chosen people of God are transferred to the proletariat, as I have frequently said. The idea of the proletariat, which does not at all correspond with the real empirical proletariat, is a mystic-messianic idea. And it is this idea of proletariat, rather than the real, empirical proletariat, which is to be endowed with the powers of dictatorship. This is a messianic dictatorship—it has nothing to do with science.

Marx was a remarkable and learned economist. But this is not the whole reason for Marxism's exclusive role in the world. This importance is explained by the religious-messianic side of Marxism. To understand Marx, we must remember that he considered the fact that the whole of human life is determined by economics, rather as an evil of the past, than as an eternal truth. In the future man is to control economics, make it subject to his will, and he will then be free. Now the leap from the realm of necessity to that of freedom, about which Marx and Engels spoke, is a messianic leap. The purely deterministic interpretation of Marxism, which was spread at the end of the XIXth century among both Marxists and their sympathizers, is a wrong interpretation. At any rate, such an interpretation is in complete contradiction to the revolutionary *volontarism* of the communists, for whom the world is plastic, and can be modelled like a bit of wax into any desired figure. It was not by accident that Marx said that whereas up to the present day philosophers had tried to comprehend the world, now they must change it and create a new world. Marxism is full of contradictions. Take, for instance, the problem of materialism. To what degree was Marx a materialist?

Marx's materialism is very questionable. The humanistic, even idealistic elements in Marx were made clearer after the publication of his *Nachlass*, specially the article on *Nazionalökonomie und Philosophie* (National Economy and Philosophy). Marx came out of the romantic epoch and out of German idealism. In his youth he was even a romantic poet. And the traces of this romanticism always remained in his style: irony, paradox, contradiction. Hegel's influence on him was was stronger than those Marxists thought, who moved away from his sources. But a certain dualism always stayed with Marx. First of all Marx condemned capitalism, as an alienation of human nature, its *Verdinglichung*, its making the labourer a thing: he condemned the inhumanity of the capitalist régime. The moral element, which Marxist doctrine denies so categorically, was very strong in Marx. The theory of surplus value, which is based on a mistaken theory of the value of labour taken from Ricardo, is first of all moral in character: it condemns exploitation. The exploitation of man by man, of class by class, was to Marx original sin. But the concept "exploitation" is moral, and not economic. A partisan of the capitalist regime, under which there surely is exploitation of the workers, might well ask why exploitation is such a bad thing, since it can aid in economic development, in the prosperity of the state, and the flowering of civilization. These arguments have, in fact, often been used by bourgeois ideologues. But exploitation is first of all a moral evil, and is subject to moral condemnation. And the Marxists, despite all their a-moral theories, are filled with the moral pathos of hatred for the exploiters. The terrible curses in which communist propaganda is so rich, are really moral judgments, and without this moral judgment, meaningless. This is one side of Marxism, concerned with man's freedom and his moral responsibility.

There is another phase, no less important. This is connected with economic determinism. Capitalism is condemned not only because it involves the moral evil of exploitation, but also because the capitalist economy has ceased to be productive, because it hinders the development of productive forces, and because it is doomed to disappear, by the necessity of history. The Marxists firmly believe that the steady movement of history will award them the victory. They condemn those forms of socialism which refuse to rely on historic necessity. From Hegel they received the belief that there is meaning in the historical process and that historic necessity leads to a messianic kingdom.

It is hard to say which of these two elements in Marxism is the stronger. And the arguments are always confused. We need to go deeper into the marxist philosophy to see that in every essential it contradicts adherence to materialism. The whole positive pathos of Marx was tied to his belief that man, the social man, could rule the world, this world of necessity, could organize a new society and put an end to the now prevailing anarchy, for the sake of the good of mankind, in the name of the increasing powers at man's disposal. Marxism was pessimistic as regards the past, and optimistic as concerns the future. Marx was faithful to the idealistic thesis of Fichte, that the subject creates the world. But with Fichte, the subject creates the world, theoretically, in thought, while with Marx the subject is supposed, actually, to accomplish this, to remake the world, radically to transfigure it. It is quite wrong to interpret Marxism in the spirit of objectivism, as the Marxists love to do, trying to prove that history is on their side. The Marxist philosophy may be understood as a philosophy of *praxis*, of action, but at the same time it values the reality of the material world on which the subject, man, operates: it revolts against idealism where victory over the necessity and authority of this world is attained only in thought. Marx's materialism must be understood in the intellectual atmosphere of the Forties of the last century, and as a reaction against abstract idealism. Marx wanted to bring the concrete man into the philosophical view of the world (*Weltanschauung*), and thought he was doing just that by affirming materialism, although materialism is abstract and the least concrete of philosophies. The intellectual atmosphere in which marxism arose no longer exists, and hence Marxism as a world-view is out of date.

In his thesis on Democritus and Epicurus, Marx took sides against Democritus, who was a partisan of mechanical materialism, and held that the cause of all movement was a push from without. Marx favoured Epicurus, who was an indeterminist. In his first theses on Feuerbach, Marx strongly criticizes the materialists of the past, because they took the standpoint of the objects and things, instead of the subject and of human activity. This thesis is anything but materialistic; it resembles rather an existentialist philosophy. Marx is constantly emphasizing man's activity, i.e. the subject, man's capacity to change the so-called world of objects, to bend it to his will. He denounces the mistaken idea that man is completely dependent on the objective world. In this connection, his doctrine of the fetishism of goods is very revealing. This false view sees material, objective reality, where really man's labour and human relations are active. Capital is not a thing quite apart from man, but rather the relationship between people in production. Here not only the objective process comes into action, but the active subject, as well. Nothing produces itself, quite by its own effort. There is no fatal necessity, there are no inalterable economic laws; these laws have only passing historical significance. Marxism tends toward the formation of an existentialist political economy, but it is not consistent, and constantly confuses two elements.

Perhaps the greatest contradiction in Marxism is that it

accepts teleology, the reasonable nature of the historical process, a meaning for history, a purpose to be realized in future society. This, quite clearly, is taken from Hegel, and it was justified by the idea that at the basis of history there is a world-spirit, reason. But this is quite unjustifiable by the materialistic understanding of history. Why should material, in the process that it produces, lead to the triumph of reason, and not of irrationality? On what is based this type of optimism? This is possible for Marxism only because into the material there is introduced reason, meaning, freedom, creative activity. But this means that the Marxist philosophy is not materialism, and that calling it thus is clearly doing violence to terminology. At any rate, it is more like hylozoism than materialism: it is even a special sort of idealism. Even the words dialectic materialism, which are a contradiction in terms, are used for propaganda purposes and not for philosophical application. There can be no such thing as dialectic materialism; there can be only a dialectic of the reason, of spirit, of consciousness. By itself, the material does not know meaning: this is revealed by dialectic, which receives it from spirit. Soviet philosophy has even invented the word "self-movement" to justify their contention that the source of all movement is not a push from outside, but inner freedom inherent in matter. It is laughable to call this materialism. The apotheosis of struggle, the exaltation of the revolutionary will, are possible only for such a non-materialistic philosophy. But there still remains the materialistic element also, which plays a negative role in the struggle against the independence of spiritual elements and values. In any case, this is monism, for which only one order of being exists: the realm of Caesar, and within this realm, dialectic movement takes place. In this process social forms may very easily be absolutized. The Marxist division of philosophical theories, specially developed by Engels, into idealism, which recognizes the primacy of consciousness over being and materialism, recognizing the primacy of being over consciousness, is quite unfounded, and belongs to the philosophical atmosphere of the 1840's. It is incomprehensible why being must of necessity be material being. In this kind of classification, St. Thomas Aquinas would have to be counted a materialist. I, too, would be classed as a materialist. Not only is marxist philosophy contradictory, but it is completely out of date: it suffers from sectarian decadence. And this, despite the fact that in Marx himself there is a strong positive and vital element, particularly in the sphere of economics.

\*
\* \*

Marxism-communism is so extraordinarily dynamic and active, because it bears all the traits of a religion. Neither scientific theory nor political practice would ever be able to play this role. We may note the following religious features of Marxism: a strict dogmatic system, despite practical flexibility; division into orthodoxy and heresy; the unchangeability of the philosophy of science; the holy scripture of Marx, Engels, Lenin and Stalin, which may only be interpreted, but may never be subject to doubt; the division of the world into two parts: the believers (the faithful) and the unbelievers (the unfaithful); the hierarchically organized Communist Church, with directives from above; the transfer of conscience to the supreme organ of the Communist Party, to a group; a totalitarianism which is characteristic only of religion; the fanaticism of the faithful; the excommunication and execution of heretics; the refusal to admit secularization within the community of the believers; the recognition of original sin (exploitation). The doctrine of the leap across from the realm of necessity into that of freedom is also religious. This is really the expectation of the transfiguration of the world and the coming of the Kingdom of God. The out-of-date *Zusammenbruchtheorie* of Marxism, which affirms that the lot of the workers will grow steadily worse, and that the whole economic system is moving toward inevitable catastrophe, reminds us of the apocalyptic explosion of the world. This theory was worked out not only by observation and analysis of the real economic process, but by an eschatological turn of thought, the expectation of the final cataclysm of this world.

The contradiction in Marxism lies also in the fact that the realm of freedom, toward which all aspirations are turned, will be the inevitable result of necessity. Here Hegelian influence is very clear. Marxism thinks of freedom as necessity, known and accepted. This is essentially a denial of freedom, which is always bound up with the existence of a spiritual element, an element which is determined by neither nature nor society. As a religion, Marxism is a secularized form of the idea of predestination. The division of history into two parts is another pseudo-religious trait of Marxism: the period before the socialist or communist revolution is only an introduction to history; the period after that is only the beginning of true history. At the basis of the Marxist religion lies a secularized, if sub-conscious, chiliasm. Outside this, the whole pathos of Marxism is meaningless. Marxists always get angry when Marxist doctrine is called a theology, but they have never been able to refute this definition. Marxists are very fond of science, they practically worship it. They believe that real science, not "bourgeois" science, will solve all problems. In this attitude toward science, they belong to the XIXth, rather than to the XXth century.

Marxist thinking is very uncritical, it is even hostile to criticism. Marxists have the same aversion to critical thinking as have orthodox theologians. The contradictions in Marxism are partly due to the fact that it is not so much a struggle against capitalist industry, as a victim of it, a victim of that power of economics over human life which we see in the societies of the XIXth and XXth centuries. In this Marxism has a passive attitude toward the social milieu in which it arose, has not carried on spiritual struggle against it. Hence for Marxism the new man, the man of the future social society, will be factory-

made. He is the child of cruel necessity and not of freedom. The dialectic of capitalist evil is to give birth to
good; the darkness in which man is deformed into a
thing, is to generate light. This is a clear denial of the
inner, spiritual man. This is extreme anti-personalism,
and communist humanism offers no escape from it.
All valuation is changed into dependence on whether
everything is defined by economics and class, or whether
spiritual, moral and intellectual forces are active.

*

*   *

To a large extent Marxism attempts to denounce the
illusions of consciousness, reflecting man's economic
bondage and the class-structure of society. It unmasks
religious illusions, metaphysical, moral, aesthetic illusions,
etc. From this view-point, actually the whole of the
spiritual culture of the past is revealed as an illusion of
consciousness which merely reflects the economic scheme
of society. Here we have a formal resemblance to
Freudian psychoanalysis, which explains man exclusively from below, out of his lower qualities and instincts.
The lower creates the higher, and the higher is recognized as an illusion. Marxism has a tendency to see
not merely illusion, but falsehood, everywhere. The
genuine reality, real life, is man's struggle, the struggle
of the social man against the elemental forces of nature
and society, i.e. economics. All the rest is only auxiliary

to economics, in which marxism sees the purpose of life; science and art are only servants of social construction. Marx was a highly cultured man, but his culture is still an "illusion" of consciousness. But in the most recent admirers of Marx, the level of culture is lowered. The cultural level is very low in Soviet Russia, where there is scarcely any true culture left: only the elementary education of the masses, and a technical civilization. The complete abolition of the "illusion" of consciousness, which denies that economics is the prime reality, would bring about the complete collapse of spiritual culture. It appears that Spirit is only an illusion of badly-organized material.

The cloudiest conception in Marxist doctrine is that of "superstructure". No one has been able to offer a clear explanation of what is meant by saying that ideology and spiritual culture are "superstructures" upon economics and the class-structure of society. All this is just as vague and ill-defined as the materialist thesis in general, which would have it that spirit is an epiphenomenon of material. Materialism has never been able to formulate this clearly: it has been expressed in various ways, each as unsubstantial as the other. Engels even admitted finally, that he and Marx had exaggerated the significance of economics. If the Marxists mean to say that the economic and class-position of men influences their ideological, intellectual, moral and spiritual life, we do not have to be either Marxists or materialists to agree, completely. All these elements are mutually interactive. I see no difficulty in admitting that there may be a bourgeois catholicism, protestantism or orthodoxy, bourgeois philosophy or morals, but you must not conclude from this that the truth of spiritual creativity lies in economics, and that there is no such thing as spiritual values apart from economics. We have already made it clear that economics belongs with the means of life and not its ends, and that economic materialism is based upon a confusion between conditions, on the one hand, and first causes, on the other. Even economics itself is not material. The idea of superstructures, which the marxists use to the point of abuse, cannot stand against any serious criticism. It offers no explanation of how material reality passes over into reality of the intellectual and spiritual order, by what means economics can turn into knowledge or moral evaluation. We may safely say that Marxism as an intellectual phenomenon, is bound up with the capitalist economy of the XIXth century, and could not exist apart from that. It was a reaction against capitalist economics. But between the process of capitalist production and the exploitation of the proletariat within it, on the one side, and Marx's thinking, on the other, there is a great gulf fixed: a leap over an abyss.

The Marxists never tire of repeating that being defines consciousness. They think this is materialism, while the idealists and the extreme spiritualists could assert this with vastly more consistency. They maintain a view which is quite out of date, identifying mental and spiritual life with consciousness. But their most important fault is that they have never attempted to explain how material being can turn into consciousness or thought. Philosophical thinkers have struggled with this problem for a thousand years, and the greatest of them did not vote for materialism, which has been defended only by second-rate and mediocre philosophers. The dogma of material being which kills consciousness, can be only a belief, but never knowledge. The subject holds primacy over society, but the subject's consciousness predicates a first idea, an original creation of God, which is not before the subject, but beyond him, and vastly deeper. Here we may make one concession to the Marxists. If it is meaningless to admit the existence of class truth and goodness, we can easily accept the existence of class falsehood and untruth. Marxism is right in its criticism of capitalism and class-economics, in its denunciation of the falsehoods of class-consciousness. But Marx attributed universal significance to certain facts which he observed in the capitalist and class-society of the XIXth century, chiefly in England. And this is a great error. It brought Marxism face to face with insoluble contradictions.

There is one fundamental difficulty in Marxism, connected with a contradiction in logic. What is, really, the Marxist theory? Is it, like all theories and ideologies, a reflection of the economic facts of its time and the class struggles then going on, that is a "superstructure" and hence subject to the normal marxist explanation? Or is it the revelation of essential truth? In the second case, a real miracle has taken place: in the middle of the XIXth century, for the first time the real truth about the process of history has been revealed, a truth which is something other than merely a "superstructure" and a reflection of economics. Either way you put it, the Marxists cannot easily accept. The first proposition makes Marxism a transient and relative theory, useful in the class-struggle, but unable to pretend that it is true: it puts Marxism on a level with all other theories and ideologies. The second, which would recognize Marxism as the revelation of essential truth, contradicts the Marxist theory itself, which refuses to admit the possibility that such kind of truth may be revealed. The Marxist's answer to this would probably be a dialectic justification of relativism. They would say that the Marxist theory is a relative truth, like all other truths, but a truth which is, all the same, very useful in the social struggle. But aside from the logical weakness of such an answer, it in no way justifies or explains the exclusive importance of Marxism, which distinguishes it from all other relative truths. It is quite clear that the idea of the unique role of Marxism is based on faith, and cannot pretend to have the least scientific significance. Marxism-communism is the religion of a sect for whom the supreme value is not the well-being of the workers, but the confession of the true faith.

There is a striking contrast between materialism and a logical realism of comprehension, which recognizes a genuine, general reality. For instance, class is more real than the concrete person; the idea of the proletariat more important than the proletariat itself. Quite naïvely and uncritically, the Marxists mistake an objectivation of basic realities for those realities themselves. Lenin's one philosophical book, written for polemic purposes, is particularly distinguished by this type of naïveté. For Lenin, objective realities are reflected in knowing. He naïvely accepts a realist hypothesis which might have been made before there was any philosophical criticism. Now this view-point of Lenin's, which even asserts absolute truth, is in serious contradiction with that of Engels, who holds that the criteria of truth are practical, that is, Engels confesses a philosophy of action. In Lenin there is no hint of the idea that truth is revealed primarily to the proletariat. This idea is found more clearly in A. Bogdanoff, who undertook to construct a purely social philosophy. Lenin is a naïve realist: that is how he understood materialism. This is in complete contradiction to other phases of Marxism. Marxism does not know a real gnosseology. In Marxism faith overshadows knowledge.

But there is another, no less important, contradiction in Marxism, this one moral rather than logical. Marxism lays great store by the a-moral or extra-moral character of its doctrine. Marx disliked ethical socialism; he considered a morally-based socialism as reactionary. Nevertheless the Marxists are constantly passing moral judgment, and especially moral condemnation. But every condemnation of the bourgeois or the capitalists, or all those whom the Marxists call social-traitors (and this includes the greater part of human-kind) is moral in its very nature. Condemnation of the exploiters is a moral judgment; outside moral evaluation it is meaningless. The very distinction between bourgeois and proletariat is axiological in nature. And the division of the world into two parts, the kingdom of light and the kingdom of darkness, is almost Manichean. Revolutionary Marxism truly includes a strong element of moral valuation and moral condemnation. In reality, the whole world comes under this moral condemnation, save only the faithful believers in Marxism-communism. The wide-spread accusation that Marxist-communists deny morals, is quite wrong. It is more correct to say that their morals are different. And on the basis of their "other" morals, we must admit that they are very great moralists. The Marxist moral standard is dualistic, and we must now look into this dualism.

It is true that Marxism is inclined to deny what is usually called a general-human, universal moral standard: it denies the moral unity of mankind. This derives from the class view-point. The Marxist moral standard is neither Christian nor humanistic, in the old meaning of that word. Marxism holds that this all-human moral standard is a sly trick of the ruling classes who are using the idea of an absolute moral norm to weaken the revolutionary class-struggle. The Marxist revolutionary (I am not speaking of revolutionary and reforming social-democracy) is convinced that he is living in a world of unbearable evil, and that in his struggle against this world of evil and darkness all means are permitted. You need waste no ceremony on the devil: he is simply to be annihilated. It would not be correct to state that for the Marxist revolutionaries everything is permissible, but they do consider as permissible any means against the enemy, which represents the realm of the devil, of exploitation, injustice, darkness and reaction. In regard to their own realm of light, justice and progress, on the contrary, they insist upon the old-style moral values of duty and sacrifice. In Soviet Russia, alongside the employment of methods which go counter to Christian or humanist moral standards, we often find an effort to implant virtue by compulsion, the insistence on moralism. The Marxist moral consciousness is torn by the contradiction between relationship with the past and present, on one hand, and with the future, on the other. As yet there is no such thing as one human-kind: the classes exist, with their rights and their interests, the exploiters and the exploited, and therefore there can be no one moral system. But in the future, after the social revolution, when the classes have disappeared, there will be one human-kind and one moral standard for all humanity. The Marxists do not so much deny an all-human morality, as they assign it to the future. And on the basis of that future, single, all-human moral standard, they judge the past and the present: they pass moral judgment. The moral contradiction lies in the fact that Marx condemned the capitalist system from the view-point of this all-human moral standard, condemned it for its inhumanity, for its making man into a thing. Here Marx uses that very all-human moral standard which he is attempting to deny.

The light of the future, all-human moral value, falls on the estimation of the present.

Marxism can no more put itself outside the moral universe, than outside universal logic. This dualism in Marxist morals is most evident in the dualism characterizing Marxist humanism. The sources of Marxism are more humane, and in the process of realizing Marxism in Soviet Russia, they are striving for humanism. But there man is crushed for the sake of man, and all his life's possibilities are terribly reduced. The process of humanizing life, especially in social organization, is accompanied by a process of dehumanization. This is due to the fact that the present is considered only as a means toward the future. The value of human life for itself in the present is denied. Marxist consciousness was seriously narrowed by the fact that it concentrated exclusively on conflict with social wrong. It is hard for the average man to contain fullness and many-sidedness in his life: he always tends to leave out many possible phases. Marx's atheism, seemingly less doubtful than his materialism, results from his exclusion of one very important phase, of man as a spiritual being. Marx followed Feuerbach, but added one new argument against religious faith. He held that faith arose from social disorganization, from man's dependence upon the forces of nature and society. He called religion opium for the people because in it he perceived one of the chief obstacles to a struggle for a better social system. A false idea of God, which degraded man, was responsible for this.

The elimination of this illusion of consciousness, toward which Marxism strives, would lead not only to a lowering of the level of spiritual culture, but probably to its complete disappearance, as something unnecessary. The vast spiritual culture of the past, the great creative movements, the great creative geniuses—all this will be recognized as the product of exploitation, in the interests of a privileged cultural layer, all based on injustice. They will say with Dostoevsky's hero, and they are saying it, "we will smother every genius in his cradle".

The greatest upthrusts of spiritual creativity have always been connected with the recognition of the existence of another world, no matter in what form this was conceived. Living only in one, would make life flat. Being shut up in the immanent circle of this world means setting a limit, the closing-off of infinity. But the creative act of the human spirit is always a yearning toward infinity, toward the transcendent, which, paradoxically, must be recognized as immanent. For me the transcendent, or the transcending, is immanent. To my finite and limited consciousness there is given a striving toward the unlimited and the infinite. Recognizing only the realm of Caesar is shutting oneself up in the finite. And this leads finally to the denial of all human creativeness. There is danger in Marxism of recognizing only economic and technical creativeness: everything must serve social construction, alone.

Marxism is right when it asserts that man is able to change the world and make it subject to himself. But on the other hand Marxism proposes subjecting ourselves to historic necessity, to the point of deifying this necessity. One of the least understandable elements in Marxism is its limitless optimism in relation to historic necessity, its boundless faith in the goodwill and meaningfulness of the historic process. This is comprehensible in Hegel: he had the world-reason and the world spirit in action, determining the meaning of events. But why could material and the material process achieve such a miracle? Even Hegel's historic optimism is neither acceptable nor justifiable: it is an extreme form of universal determinism, denying the action of human freedom in history. This is less justified in Marxism. It contradicts the Marxist faith that man can change the world. Marxist historic optimism is a secularized form of messianic faith. Faith in automatic progress is always that. But truth is beyond both optimism and pessimism. The historic process is more tragic: in it several elements are active. The Marxist optimistic faith in the beneficence of the process of history is a secularized experience of faith in Providence. But even the old faith in Providence needs reassessment: it involved optimism and a non-tragic concept of this world of phenomena, a world subject to necessary causal relationships.

There is a measure of truth in Marxism, and this we must recognize. We must recognize the necessity of a social revolution in the world. We may only hope that this revolution will be less cruel and violent than the Marxists predict. But Marxism in its historic form is dangerous for the realm of spirit which, in the course of history, has been threatened in various forms at various times. Intellectually Marxism is not at all creative. Marxist thinking is very poor. It denies variety, and creates simply a dull grey boredom. Marxist thought is not at all on the level of Marx, himself. But this does not prevent, rather even helps, its playing a very active role. This strength in Marxism is partly due to the weakness of Christians, to the lack of expression of the realm of Spirit, which too often gives way to the realm of Caesar.

# CHAPTER IX

# NATIONALISM AND THE UNITY OF MANKIND

To what extent does the unity of mankind really exist? National unity insists upon recognition in a far greater degree than does the unity of mankind. This national unity is revealed particularly in time of war. Philosophically, this presents a complex problem of realities which cannot be recognized as personalities. One human-kind is not an entity, not a sort of personality of some higher hierarchical rank: it has no existential centre; in its super-personal reality it is not capable of joy or of suffering. But one human-kind is not only an abstraction of thought, it represents a certain level of reality in human life, a high quality of man: his all-inclusive humanity. The quality of nationality depends on the humanity revealed in it. There are two tendencies in the history of human life: one toward individualization, and the other toward universalism. Nationality is a degree of individualization as regards humanity, and a union, as regards man. Nationality as a degree of individualization in the life of society, is a complex historical development: it is determined not by blood alone (the race is zoology, prehistoric material), but by language, as well: not only by geography, but first and foremost by a common historical fate. Nationality is an individual quality of man, individual both in the relationships of mankind and those of man. A self-asserting nationality may take the form of nationalism, i.e. exclusiveness and hostility toward other nationalities. This is a disease affecting nationality, much in evidence in our day. Over against nationalism, men have tried to set internationalism, which is another disease. Internationalism is abstract and poverty-stricken, not the concrete oneness of human-kind which includes within itself all degrees of national individuality, but an abstract unity which negates national individuality.

Internationalism was a clear error of Marxism, rejected by life itself, circulation within an abstraction. Against nationalism must be set up universalism which does not deny national individualizations, but unites them in a concrete one-ness. Universalism is the affirmation of national life and values. All great peoples, with their own idea and their special calling in the world, have attained universal significance through the high achievements of their cultures. Dante, Tolstoi, Shakespeare and Goethe are alike both national and universal. Temptations, broken relationships and distortions are as highly characteristic of national life, as they are of the life of individuals. Imperialism is one such temptation and distortion. Large nations united in great states, are taken ill with the will to power. The tendency to imperialism is implicit in the formation of national states. And the final dimension of this imperialistic will to power is its tendency to form a world-empire. Such were the Empire of the Ancient East, the Roman Empire, that of Charlemagne, the

Byzantine Empire. As regards its pretensions, so was the Russian Empire and that of Napoleon. An emperor, in distinction from czars and kings, is a world-emperor, and every empire is, in intention, a world-empire. Such was the false and meaningless pretension of pan-germanism. Imperialism is a distorted expression of the striving for world-union, for the one-ness of all mankind. Dostoevsky felt keenly this thirst for general unity and saw the temptations resulting from it. The nationalism of small peoples is a manifestation of isolation and of self-satisfaction. The nationalism of great peoples is imperialist expansion. In the nationalism of great peoples there is a fatal dialectic.

The individual value of nationality is expressed above all in its culture, and not in its state-form. The state, with which nationalism allies itself, is anything but original, or individual. All states very much resemble each other in their organization of an army, the police, finances, international politics. And very often state nationalism turns out to be not national at all. This was evident in fascism. Nationalism is inseparably bound to the state and values much more highly the state, which is often quite devoid of individual national qualities, than a truly national culture. The literature and the music of any people is far more individual than its army and its police, which are part of international technics. The consequence is that nationality is a positive value enriching the life of mankind, which without this would be an abstraction: on the other hand, nationalism is an evil, egoistic self-assertion, it is scorn and even hatred for other peoples. Nationalism, in sharp distinction to patriotism, gives birth to chauvinism and xenophobia. The most terrible thing about nationalism is that it is one of the causes of war.

\*

\* \*

The emotional life which is connected with nationality is very complex and confused. Human emotions and passions are objectivized. The rise of the so-called collective, super-personal realities, is explained in a large measure by this objectivation, this throwing-out and exteriorization of strong emotions. In this way both nationalism and patriotism are created, both of which, despite Marx, play a gigantic roie in history. In patriotism emotional life is more immediate and natural, and it is expressed chiefly in love for one's homeland, one's country, one's people. Patriotism is unquestionably a real emotional value: it needs no rationalization. The complete absence of patriotism is abnormal, a defective condition. Nationalism, on the other hand, is less natural and represents a certain degree of the rationalization of emotional life. Nationalism ties itself closely to the state, and hence becomes a cause of war. Nationalism involves more of hatred to the stranger than love of one's own. And nationalist passions which are plaguing the world are not primary, immediate passions; they grow together with national interests: very often they are called forth by propaganda. So-called selfish national interests are not immediate and egoistic: there has already taken place an exteriorization and objectivation of egoist interests and passions, and their transfer to collective realities. The same thing occurs with class interests, which may even contradict personal and egoistic interests. Man easily becomes the victim and the slave of such collective realities, which are produced by an exteriorization of his emotional, often egoistic condition. A man often defends such interests, not only egoistically, but even unselfishly. And in the unselfish, he may be worse than in the selfish. This is specially evident in the rise of wars, for instance. Nationalism plays a large part in causing wars: it creates an atmosphere of war. But nationality may be debased and destroyed in war, which is often caused by national passions and interests, sometimes selfish, sometimes not.

The outbreak of war is most interesting: it always presupposes an atmosphere of insanity. The capitalist order has a special capacity for causing wars. A group of capitalists may desire war for the sake of a market, or for oil, or something else. This group of capitalists can be not only crushed, economically, but physically destroyed, either by war or by revolution which is easily produced after a war. Personal courage does not inspire wars, which are entered upon out of selfish motives. Nevertheless the madness of passion, or of the very interests themselves, may urge on a war. War is always the product of fate (*fatum*) and not of freedom. Although in the past war might be considered a relative evil, and although an offensive war may never be justified, a war of defence or of liberation is justifiable. But the time will come when war will be absolute evil, an evil madness. Such is our epoch, in every way determined by two world wars and the fear of a third. Hence we must battle against nationalism and against degenerated capitalism. We must strive by all means to affirm federalism, to unite humanity on a basis which is beyond the state: the state has been a self-sufficient power, sucking the people's blood. War has led to an unbelievable increase in the power and importance of the state. Socialism has become monstrously etatistic. This is the sickness of our time. The state, or even war, is becoming quite autonomous: they refuse to submit to any moral or spiritual element. The national state and war both act automatically. War is not declared by men or peoples, but by its own automatically acting force. And it is surprising that the boundless suffering of shattered peoples does not produce a general strike against war. This only proves that in certain moments the fate of peoples is determined by fanaticism and madness. Instead of a function and a means to an end, the state becomes an end in itself and an imagined reality. There is no more vicious idea than the sovereignty of national states, embraced by the peoples to their own destruction. A federation of peoples presupposes the denial of this idea of national sovereignty. We might propose to exchange the word "nation" for the word "people". It should here be added, that if nationalism is a negative phenomenon, racism is an absolute falsehood. The ancient Hebrew racism had some meaning, being based on religion, but it can take definitely negative forms. The racist myth, as it is asserted by the German ideology, is an evil emanation of the will to power and to tyranny. It is many times worse than nationalism.

It is astonishing what great misfortunes of men and peoples are caused by a false objectivation, the alienation of human nature in some external and collective pseudo-reality. Man lives by collective consciousness, by the myths he has created, which then become powerful realities, directing his whole life. Social psychopathy is vastly more powerful than social psychology. The formation of pseudo-realities plays a great role in historic life. The abstraction of unhealthy thinking gives birth to myth, myth becomes reality which upsets history. Hence the problem of the real forces in history is so complex. Marxist realism also deals with abstract ideas which have become transformed into myths.

The world is divided not only into nations, but into larger unities: the Latin world, the Anglo-Saxon world, the Germanic or the Slavic worlds. We are constantly using these expressions, although their meaning is not very clear. At all events, race is not a scientific term: we cannot speak scientifically of races. This is the history of the world. Scientifically, the most important division is into East and West. They even talk of the East and the West fronts. The self-satisfied and humanistic culture of the West tends to consider its type of culture universal and unique, it does not recognize the existence of various types of culture, does not wish to be complemented by other worlds. This same self-satisfaction and exclusivity may be noted in Western Europe as in the smallest nationalities. The division of the world into East and West has a universal-historic significance. More than any other it is related to the problem of attaining the planetary unity of all mankind. The consciousness of the Christian Middle Ages held the idea of universal unity, but the union of East and West in this sense was not attained. The East (I am not speaking of the Russian East) remained for a long time outside the dynamic of history. Only those peoples which had been gained for Christianity have been historically dynamic. But two world wars have changed the course of history. We are now witnessing the active entry into world-history of the East. The European West has ceased to have a monopoly on culture. While the human world is falling apart, we are at the same time entering the universal epoch. East and West must come at last to unity, but this will arrive by the way of disagreements and divisions which will appear even greater than the former contrasts.

Nationalism does not include the universal idea. Universalism, by the way, always includes messianism. The ancient Hebrew messianism is a prototype of messianism universal in significance. Universalism is inherent in Russian messianism, which differs greatly from nationalism. But higher elements become distorted and deformed in history. This is happening, now, to

Russian messianism, which is degenerating into imperialism and even nationalism. The messianic idea of Moscow the third Rome served as the ideological basis for a great and powerful state. But the will to power has deformed the messianic idea. Neither the earlier "Moscow" Russia nor Imperial Russia were able to realize the idea of a third Rome. At the base of Soviet Russia, also, lay the messianic idea, but it, again, was distorted by the will to power. The realm of Spirit has always tended to take on the forms of Caesar's realm. Messianism has always been transferred to the realm of Caesar, when it should have been attached to the realm of Spirit, the Kingdom of God. We are faced with the question, in what form and to what degree is Christian messianism possible—messianism after the appearance of the Messiah, Christ? Conservative Christians, their attention turned toward the past, deny the possibility of Christian messianism, as well as the prophetic side of Christianity in general. But still there is in Christianity the messianic expectation of Christ's second coming in power and glory, the messianic seeking for the Kingdom of God on earth as it is in heaven, the possible expectation of a new era of the Holy Spirit. The very development and realization of a universal Church is a messianic expectation. In this lies the significance of the ecumenical movement for the rapprochement of Churches and confessions. The Church universal, which knows neither East nor West, is the spiritual basis for the unity of mankind. At the same time mankind is more and more divided, demons and evil spirits have been set at liberty, which are creating chaos. And this developing chaos leads, not to freedom, but to tyranny. Overcoming the prevalent national currents is one of the great tasks of our time. A federation of peoples, the abandonment of national-state sovereignty is the way to this end. But this predicates spiritual and social changes in human society. By themselves, political and social solutions are powerless. The spiritual revolution which must take place in the world, and which is actually in progress, goes farther and deeper than social revolutions.

# CHAPTER X

# THE NEW MAN. THE ETERNAL MAN

FOR US THE MOST important question is the question of man. Everything proceeds from him, and to him everything returns. We hear much about the appearance of the new man. He is being searched for, everywhere. This is nothing new: it has happened, often, before. Unquestionably, man is in the process either of progress or regression; he is not standing still. We may speak of the new technical man, of the Fascist man, of the Soviet, or the communist man. We even hear expressions like the catholic or the protestant man, the Renaissance or the romantic man. You may give a host of names to new types of men, but man himself changes less than would seem to be the case from his appearance and his gestures: often he has only changed his clothes, putting on in one period a revolutionary suit, in another the costume of a reactionary; he may seem to be a romantic, or a classic, without being either, inwardly.

The idea of the new man, the new Adam, of re-birth, is a Christian idea: the antique world had no knowledge of it. The pre-Christian world knew this idea only in a superficial form. There was a time when the appearance of the possibility of a sense of sin, of repentance, offered a starting point for developing a really new man. But now we have again lost our capacity for repentance. Reversals in social position, when the rich become poor and the poor rich, by themselves do not make man inwardly different. Man may improve or deteriorate, within the limits of his own type, but this does not form a new man. It must be said that political revolutions, even the most radical of them, change man comparatively little. We hear much of the great difference between the bourgeois and the communist man, but the victorious communist, once he has got into power, may be inwardly and spiritually, to the very marrow of his bones, a bourgeois. Spiritual bourgeoisie is very characteristic both of socialists and communists. It is characteristic of everyone who too greatly desires a comfortable situation here in this world, of anyone to whom the infinite remains a closed book, and who clings firmly to the finite. Only a new birth, the birth of spiritual man, who so long has slumbered and been held down, may be the real appearance of a new man. Change, development, demand a subject of development. There is no development without someone or something which develops.

The error of the XIXth century theory of evolution lay in the fact that it derived the subject of development from development itself. Thus it remained a surface theory. They talked about how development occurred. There is a certain relationship between phases of development. A man may develop to a great extent, but he still remains that same man. If a quite new subject, a new personality appeared as the result of development, that would not have been development. Personality implies a union of change with changelessness. When there occurs not only a change in personality, but treason to it, personality deteriorates, but that is the only change. A new man, something new within man, predicates that man continues to exist, in his human quality. No alteration, no matter how important, can make a man out of an ape. The Nietzschean idea of the superman is a yearning for something higher, but it is betrayal of man and of humanity. This is talk of the rise of a new kind, a new race, divine, diabolic, or just animal. But not of the new man. The new man is connected with the eternal man, with the eternal in man.

In the new man there is hidden not only the eternal man Adam Kadmon, but the old man, the old Adam. In the depths of man's sub-conscious there is everything: the primitive man is there—not yet completely overcome; in the sub-conscious there is the animal world, just as in the whole of history. Consciousness plays a dual role; it both widens and narrows, sets limitations. Even in the most radical of revolutions, the past retains its power over man. The old instincts of violence, cruelty and love of power are active in revolutions. These are revealed in strong reaction against the past. The people of the French Revolution were men of the old régime. This must be said of the Russian Revolution as well. In the veins of its actors there was still the blood of slaves. The terror in

revolutions is an old, not a new element in them. No
revolution can form the wholly new man in a short
time, although it introduces something new. Revolution is a phenomenon of the old régime: in itself it
is not a new world. The most powerful element in
revolutions is the negative reaction to the preceding
régime, and in revolution hatred is always stronger than
love.

Economics is, of all elements, least capable of creating
the new man. Economics relates to the means and not the
ends of life, and when it is made an end, man's degradation proceeds apace. It is quite untrue to say that the new
Soviet man is a collective man, and lives collectively,
whereas the old intellectual was an individualist. The
conflict of collectivism against individualism is a regular
mystification. In the great majority of cases, the old intelligentsia lived in the collective, and its ways of thinking
were collective. The man of the past was far more collec-
tivist than individualist. Those persons who thought or
judged individually were extremely rare. What Heidegger
calls "*das* Man" always prevailed: this is collectivism
which is not a primitive reality, but a fictitious, illusory
product of consciousness. In the so-called period of
construction, the Soviet man really does reveal some
new traits which sharply distinguish him from the old
intelligentsia. The old intelligentsia was revolutionary in
type: it lived in schism from the surrounding world. The
new Soviet intelligentsia is not at all revolutionary: it is
humble and obedient. From it is demanded the virtue of

constructiveness, above all in the economic sphere. The old intelligentsia lived exclusively in the future and often in a dreamy unreal relation to it. The new Soviet intelligentsia lives in the present. The process taking place in the new Soviet man is not only a terrible reduction of freedom, but the very taste for freedom is disappearing, even the comprehension of what freedom really is. Once they became conquerors and bosses, the old revolutionaries, themselves, changed beyond all recognition. But this does not in the least mean that the new man has made his appearance, it is only a return to the old man. It is not true that the old left-wing intelligentsia was divided, and soft, and inactive: the whole history of the revolutionary movement proves the contrary. The heroism of the old revolutionary intelligentsia, and the sacrifices they made, forms the blood-stained capital on which the bolsheviks are living to-day. But some new traits have appeared which must be recognized as the result, not of revolution, but of war. A militaristic type of man has developed, which was not known previously, but he is not the new man. In the course of history, human types have often changed. And during almost every decade of the XIXth and XXth centuries, in Russia, some have pretended that the new man had appeared. And the change was usually from a gentler to a more cruel type of person. The idealists of the Forties were more gentle than the realists of the Sixties, the *Narodniks* were softer than the Marxists, the Mensheviks than the Bolsheviks, and the revolutionary Bolsheviks less cruel than the constructive-Bolsheviks. These changes usually took place through psychological reaction, but in reality the new man did not appear. The arrival in history of the technical man presents a greater novelty. And this is a most disturbing phenomenon, which throws some light on the possibility, itself, of the birth of the new man.

*<br>*    *

The historic fate of peoples is deeply tinged with revolution. It is surprising that there are still people who idealize the idea of revolution, and are ready to accept the coming revolution as the triumph of all that is good and beautiful. But all revolutions, without exception, reveal the extraordinary baseness of human nature in the great majority, alongside the heroism of a few individuals. Revolutions are the children of fate, and not of freedom. And to understand revolution, we must understand the element of fate in it. In a large degree, revolutions are payments of the debts of the past, a sign that creative spiritual forces for reforming society were wanting. Hence we cannot expect revolution to produce the new man. The avenger of past wrongs is not a new creature, he is still the old man. Revolution is a word with many meanings, and it has been terribly misused by attributing various meanings to the word. If you take the word revolution as meaning the acts of violence, murder and blood-

shed at a given date in history, if you understand it as
meaning the suppression of all liberty, concentration
camps, etc., then you cannot desire revolution, neither
can you expect it to produce the new man: you can only,
under certain conditions, see it as a fateful necessity, and
hope its violence may be mitigated. If, on the other hand,
you think of revolution as the radical alteration of the
very bases of human society and of the relationships
among men, then you should both desire and prepare for
it. But the idolatry of revolution is just as false as any
other idolatry. In any case, profound and radical change
and improvement do not depend upon the degree of
bloodshed and violence. If the revolutionary is the
new man, then Gandhi is more a revolutionary than
Lenin and Stalin. The appearance of the truly new man,
and not merely a change of clothes, presupposes spiritual
movement and change. Without an inner, spiritual
nucleus, and the creative processes in it, no new social
order can produce the new man. Materialism recognizes
only the external, and denies the internal. The materialists do not even understand what the words mean when
we speak of the inner life, or the spiritual life. They are
like blind men who cannot see the beauty of colour.
The corrective to mechanistic materialism—the idea of
atomic movement caused by a push from without—
adduced by dialectic materialism, is of no help, whatever.
Man remains a being wholly determined by nature and
the social milieu.

But there is another side to revolution, connected

with time. Revolution sings *du passé faisons table rase*. The
essence of revolution is the radical destruction of the past.
But this is an illusion of revolution: the furious destruction of the past is still the past, and not the future. And
only the decadent, decaying and evil past can be
destroyed: not those elements in it which are true and
eternally valuable. Idealizing the past is just as false as
idealizing the future. True value is independent of time,
it belongs to eternity. And there is a danger that the new
man may be an outcast, alien to himself, oriented only
toward the material side of life, toward technical civilization. It is astonishing how closely the new Soviet man
seems to resemble the new man of such a hostile world
as is America. This type of the technical, productive
man is just as likely to be born of communism as of
capitalism. The most positive traits of the Russian,
which revolution has brought forth, his unusual
readiness for sacrifice, his endurance of suffering, his
communal spirit, are all Christian virtues developed
in the Russian people by Christianity, that is by the
past.

The communist traits of the new man, born less from
freedom than from destiny, are repulsive, rather than
attractive. This new man worships the ideal or the idol
of productivity, which makes man a function of production; he worships power and success; he is merciless
toward the weak; he is moved by competition in struggle,
and still more important, there is going on in him a process of weakening the spiritual, almost to the point of

extinction. The new man tries to close off the infinite in his nature and to take shelter under the finite. The new communist man is of this world, he denies the other. Most of all, he prides himself that he is freed from the transcendent. This means that the new man wants to live entirely in the realm of Caesar, and to break completely with the realm of Spirit. He is a monist, and in this lies his basic error. He is not at all a new man: he is only another one of the transformations of the old Adam with all his old instincts.

The whole world will have to undergo a social reconstruction, through an intense period of material construction. This process will involve concentrated attention to the material side of human life, and a still greater degree of organization. But this is no guarantee that the new man will appear—it may all go on under the sign of the old Adam. This old Adam will be more social: he will have to be socialized. This is a process which has already occurred in various forms, in the history of human society. And this process will not bring about the disappearance of the bourgeois, the citizen of the realm of Caesar. It will only produce a more just and equal sharing of the bourgeois qualities. This justice, at least, is something to be hailed as acceptable. But it is not the last word. Man has always tended to mistake the means of life for its ends. And the so-called new man of the age, of to-morrow, will be even more inclined to think that the means of life are its final goal. The true purpose of life will be hidden from him. Hence he will consider himself a collective man, and in this he will perceive real novelty.

But after the necessary process of socialization there will begin that of individualization. Without this, man as a personality will disappear. But man's inner spirituality cannot be suppressed, no matter how cruelly necessity presses upon him; man's thirst for the spiritual will assert itself. We shall see, in the next chapter, what an important element in all this is the problem of death.

The eternal man, oriented toward eternity and infinity, is at once the eternally new man and an eternal and limitless purpose. The eternal man is not something given once for all: he is not to be comprehended statically. The truly new man is a realization of the eternal man, bearing in himself the image and likeness of God. In man there is a divine basis, *Grund*, about which Tauler has spoken so well. Hence looking forward to the future involves those parts of the past which were eternal. Man's dignity demands that he shall not become a slave to swift-running time. The new man must be creative, and hence he must look toward the future, toward that which has never been. This is his answer to the call of God. But creativity cannot be identified with work. Work belongs to the kingdom of necessity ("In the sweat of thy brow shalt thou earn thy bread"); it belongs to the realm of Caesar. The dignity of labour must be upheld: hence the central importance of the workers, hence the necessity of ending the exploitation of labour. This is the religious truth of socialism. But creativeness belongs to the purposes of life, to the realm of freedom, which is that of Spirit. We dare not subject the purposes of life, its ends, to life's means: freedom cannot be subjected to necessity: the realm of Spirit cannot be subordinated to that of Caesar. Hence the religious truth in personalism.

# CHAPTER XI

# THE TRAGEDY OF HUMAN EXISTENCE: UTOPIA: THE SPHERE OF THE MYSTIC

THE MORE INTELLECTUAL Marxists affirm that they have overcome and destroyed the tragedy in human existence, and that unlike Christianity, they have accomplished this without resort to myth. This is probably Marxism's greatest pretension. But they are fooling themselves when they think they can get along without myth; they are saturated with myth, as has already been said. Marxism is not a social utopia: the experiment of realizing Marxism in social life is possible. But Marxism is a spiritual utopia, an utopia of the complete rationalization of the whole of human life, pretending, just because it claims to overcome the tragedy in human life, to answer all the questionings of the human spirit. This claim to overcome the tragedy in the life of men is possible, only because man has become an outcast, a stranger from himself. The lowest and most pitiful of these pretensions is that the tragedy of death, chief tragedy in human existence, has been overcome. This is accomplished by banishing the thought of death, the *memento mori*, through final submergence of the individual in the life of the collective, submergence to the point of extinguishing personal consciousness. The reality is just the reverse of what the Marxists say, and on what they reckon. A more

just and perfect social order will make human life more
tragic—not outwardly, but inwardly tragic. The tragic
conflicts of the past arose from poverty, the insecurity of
life, from class or caste prejudices, from an unjust and
humiliating social order, from a denial of freedom. These
tragic contradictions can be overcome. The tragic conflicts of Antigone and Creon were related to the social
order and to social prejudices, just as were the tragic
situations of Romeo and Juliette, or the drama of Tristan
and Isolde. It may even be affirmed that the tragedy of
human life in a pure form has never been known, since
in all the tragedy of the past conflict due to the social
order or to prejudices deriving from it, have played too
important a role. When a lover cannot have the one he
loves because they belong to different classes, or because
there is too great a difference in their material circum-
stances, or the parents put inescapable obstacles in the
way, this may be very tragic, but it is not the expression
of the inner tragedy of human life, in its pure form. Pure
inner tragedy appears when there is an inevitable tragism
deriving from the nature of love itself, apart from the
social milieu in which the lovers are called to live. The
external sources of tragic conflicts may be removed by a
more just and more free social order, which overcomes
the prejudices of the past. But then, and then only, man
will be faced with the pure tragedy of life. Under a
socialist order, life's tragedy is greatly increased. The
social struggle which has hindered man from thinking
about his fate and about the meaning of his existence is

stilled, and then man will be faced with the tragedy of death, the tragic in love, the tragedy of the vanity of everything in this world. All the tragedy of life arises from the conflict of the finite with the infinite, of the temporal with the eternal, from the lack of harmony between man as a spiritual being and man as a thing of nature, living in a natural world. Here no perfection of the social order can help: it only brings out these conflicts and discords into clearer view. And the greatest, the final tragedy is that of man's attitude toward God. That optimistic and tragedy-less theory of progress, which the Marxists also share, is itself a tragedy of death-dealing time, inescapable in its final contradictions, because it makes man into a means for some future end. This tragedy can be overcome only in the Christian belief in resurrection.

*<br>*   *

Utopias have played a great role in history. These must not be confused with utopian novels. Utopias may become a motive power, more real than other more reasonable and more moderate tendencies. Bolshevism was considered a utopia, but it turned out to be more real than capitalist and liberal democracy. Utopias are usually thought to be unrealizable. This is an error: utopias not only can be realized in most cases, but they are. Utopias have been judged by the perfect schemes invented by Thomas More, by Campanella, Cabet and others, by the fantasies of Fourrier. But utopia is something deeply implicit in human nature: human nature cannot get along without utopias. Wounded and beaten by the evil in the world about him, man needs to imagine, to call forth a picture of a perfect and harmonious order for social life. Proudhon on the one hand, and Marx on the other, must be considered just as much utopians, as Saint-Simon and Fourrier. J.-J. Rousseau, also, was an utopian. Utopias have always been realized in a distorted form. The Bolsheviks are utopians: they are possessed by the idea of a perfect, harmonious order. But they are also realists, and in this capacity they are realizing their utopia in a distorted shape. Utopias are realizable, but only and inevitably in a mutilated form. But even from these imperfect and distorted utopias something positive always remains.

What are the essential elements in utopias? What are their contradictions, and what do we fail to take sufficiently into account in dealing with them? Not, I think, their unrealizability: the vision of future harmony is doubtless one of the chief qualities of an utopia. Man lives in a shattered world and dreams of a world that is whole. Wholeness is the chief sign of an utopia. Utopias has to overcome divisions and realize integrity. Utopia is always totalitarian, and totalitarianism is always utopian under the conditions of our world. This is related to the most important question of freedom. Essentially, utopia is always hostile to freedom. The utopias of Thomas More, Campanella and Cabet leave no room whatever for freedom. It may seem paradoxical to say that the most unrealizable utopia is freedom, free life. Freedom predicates that life is not finally regulated and rationalized, that there is evil in it which has to be conquered by the free exertion of the spirit. And the social utopias fail to reckon with these free efforts. Harmony and perfection are not to be realized by means of freedom. Here we face the paradox of the movement of history. Irrational forces are at work in history, and the partisans of reasonableness never take them sufficiently into account. But these irrational, elemental forces may take on forms of extreme rationalization. This is characteristic of revolution. Revolutions are always a result of the explosion of irrational forces. And at the same time, revolutions are always carried on under the sign of rational ideas, and totalitarian rational doctrines. What is called the madness of revolutions, is a rational madness. The myth which drives a revolution is usually a rational myth, involving faith in the triumph of social reason, in a rational utopia. The motive power of such a rational myth is enormous. As has already been said, revolutions are dualist in their nature, and so is the revolutionary myth.

It may be equally well said of revolutions that they are both realizable and unrealizable. They are so thoroughly realizable that once they are started, it is almost impossible to stop them. And they are unrealizable because they never attain that for which the first generation of revolutionaries, who made them, strove. It is always so. This does not mean that revolutions always take place in a vacuum, and are really only an effervescence of human passions. Revolutions form a great part of the experience of peoples, and they have left ineffaceable social consequences. But these were not at all what the authors dreamed. A successful revolution is always a failure. All the religious revolutions in history, perhaps most of all Christianity, must be considered failures. Hence we must take a dual attitude toward revolution. We cannot worship it like a divinity. Social utopias always involve falsehood, and at the same time man, in his historic destiny cannot get on without them: they are his motive forces. The revolutionary myth always involves subconscious deceit; and yet, without a revolutionary myth, you cannot make a revolution. Hence history involves inescapable tragedy.

What is the error in social utopias? Why is it that they realize something quite other than what had been intended by those who struggled and made such terrible sacrifices? The social utopia of Marx, no less than that of Fourrier, contains the idea of a perfect, harmonious state of society, that is, the faith that the realm of Caesar can be such a state. This is a radical error. Only the Kingdom of God, the realm of Spirit, can be perfect and harmonious, not the realm of Caesar. Such a perfect realm is conceivable only eschatologically. A perfect and harmonious order in the realm of Caesar would annihilate freedom, which means that such an order is not attainable in this world. Socialism must be understood from this view-point. Socialism is a social utopia, and it is based on a messianic myth. In this sense it will never be realized within the limits of this world, in the realm of Caesar. But on the other hand, socialism is a stern and prosaic reality, a necessity at a certain hour in history. In this sense, besides being utopian, and a myth, socialism is a very elemental thing: the removal of ugly exploitation and unbearable class inequality. Hence we may say that the world is entering a social epoch. Even those who do not believe in utopia and myth, so necessary for struggle, must recognize this. The socialist society which results from this movement will be neither perfect nor harmonious, nor free of contradictions. The tragedy in human life will increase, but will become deeper, something more inward. New and quite different contradictions will appear. The struggle will continue, but along new lines: for then the main struggle for freedom and individuality will begin. The reign of the bourgeois lower middle classes will be intensified and all its benefits will be generally distributed. Then must come an intense spiritual struggle against this reign of the lower social order. The struggle for social justice must continue, regardless of the forms which Caesar's realm may take: in any case these forms will be bourgeois, and in any case cannot fail to limit the freedom of Spirit. The final triumph of the realm of Spirit, which can never be a denial of social justice, presupposes a change in the structure of human consciousness, i.e. overcoming the world of objectivation. This can be envisaged only eschatologically. But the struggle against the force of objectivation, that is the power of Caesar, must take place within the limits of the realm of objectivation, and man cannot simply refuse to recognize these limits and turn away from them. Here we approach the final sphere of the mystic, to which I hope to devote a separate book. False forms of the mystic are appearing in our world, and these must be unmasked. Along with these we still have the old mystic forms, and as yet very few of us are attentive to the new mystic of the future.

*
* *

There are various forms of the mystic. The word may be used in a broader or a narrower sense. The word is used in France, to-day, in such a broad sense, that it is losing its old meaning. The same is true of the word "revolution". But in all cases the sphere of the mystic is a final phase, beyond the limits of the objective and the objectivized world. Many types of the mystic have existed in the past. Christianity has used the word in the more strict sense, to indicate that way of the spirit which led to a union with God. Writing in the first half of the XIXth century, Görres, in his many-volumed work on mysticism, proposed the distinction of three classes: divine, natural and diabolical mysticism. In this I cannot follow Görres. But we may give a definition of mysticism, which comprehends all its various forms. It is that spiritual experience which goes beyond the contrast of subject and object, i.e. is not subject to the power of objectivation. In this lies the essential difference between mysticism and religion. In religions (of various types) spiritual experience is objectivized, socialized and organized. This suggested definition covers false mysticism as well, which is a state of men's consciousness which refuses to admit the existence of God or of Spirit. This is specially true of the mystic of collectivism, which plays a large part in our present world. The most important element in the communist mystic is that it is a mystic of a messianic type: it goes beyond the limits of the objective world, which can be scientifically studied. It is based on a collective experience, in which there is no contrasting of subject with object. This is a characteristic type of false mysticism. Just as false is the old mystic of a consecrated monarchy: just as false, too, is the later but still outdated myth of the Rousseau-Jacobin democracy. Equally false is the naturalist, Dionysean type of mysticism, which would remove the conflict between subject and object, not from above, but from below. This type of mysticism is not super-rational, but irrational; not super-conscious, but unconscious. It would plunge us into the abyss. The false doctrines of collectivism-naturalism or socialism, in which man's image and personality disappear, may give rise to various forms of mysticism. True mysticism is spiritual and means spiritual experience in which man is not oppressed by objectivation.

Orthodox theological doctrines objectivize grace, and consider it a power coming from above, from without.

But for mysticism grace is a revelation from the depths, from the very bases of the divine element in man. Objectivized grace still leaves us with the contradiction between subject and object. The mystical spiritual experience is symbolized in organized religion. And it is most important to understand this symbolic character of religion: this understanding will lead to spiritual deepening. Ecstasy, which is considered characteristic of certain types of mysticism, is a passage out beyond the division between subject and object. It is communion, not with the general and objectivized world, but with the basic realities of the world of the spirit. Ecstasy is always a passage beyond everything which enslaves or oppresses—it is a passage out into freedom. This mystical outward movement is a spiritual condition and a spiritual experience. Any mysticism which does not mean a deepened spirituality, is false: such are the collective forms of mysticism, cosmic or social.

We may distinguish three types of mysticism, in the past: the mysticism of individual souls' approach to God. This is the most churchly form. Second, gnostic mysticism which must not be confused with the gnostic heretics of the first Christian centuries: this is a mysticism involving not only the individual soul, but cosmic and divine life, as well. Third, we have prophetic and messianic mysticism; this is super-historical and eschatological, the beginning of the end. And each of these three types of mysticism has its limits.

The world is moving through darkness toward a new

spirituality and a new mysticism. In it there will be no more of the ascetic world-view which turned away from the pluralities and the individualities of the world. In it ascesis will be merely a method and the means to purification. Although addressed to the world and to men, the new mysticism will not consider this objectivized world as final reality. It will be at once more involved with the world, and more free from it. This is a process of spiritual deepening. The prophetic-messianic element will be strong in the new mysticism, and in it will be revealed a true gnosis which will avoid the cosmic temptations of the ancient gnostics. And all the tormenting contradictions and divisions will be resolved in the new mysticism, which will be deeper than religions, and ought to unite them. At the same time this will be the victory over false forms of social mysticism, the victory of the realm of Spirit over that of Caesar.

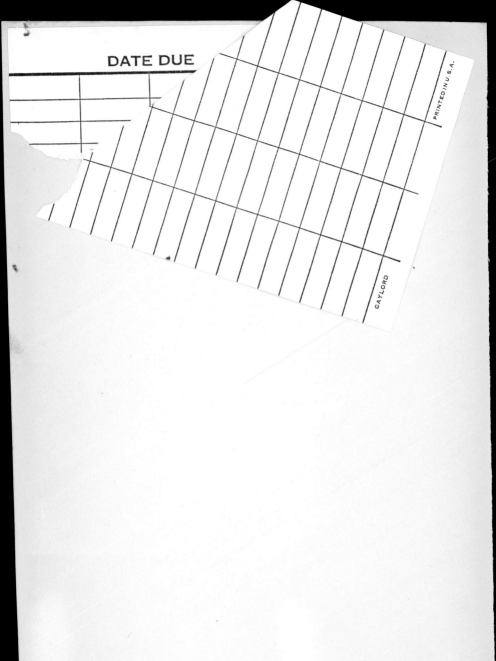